Unleashed
and Ready to Empower

Trina R. Olson

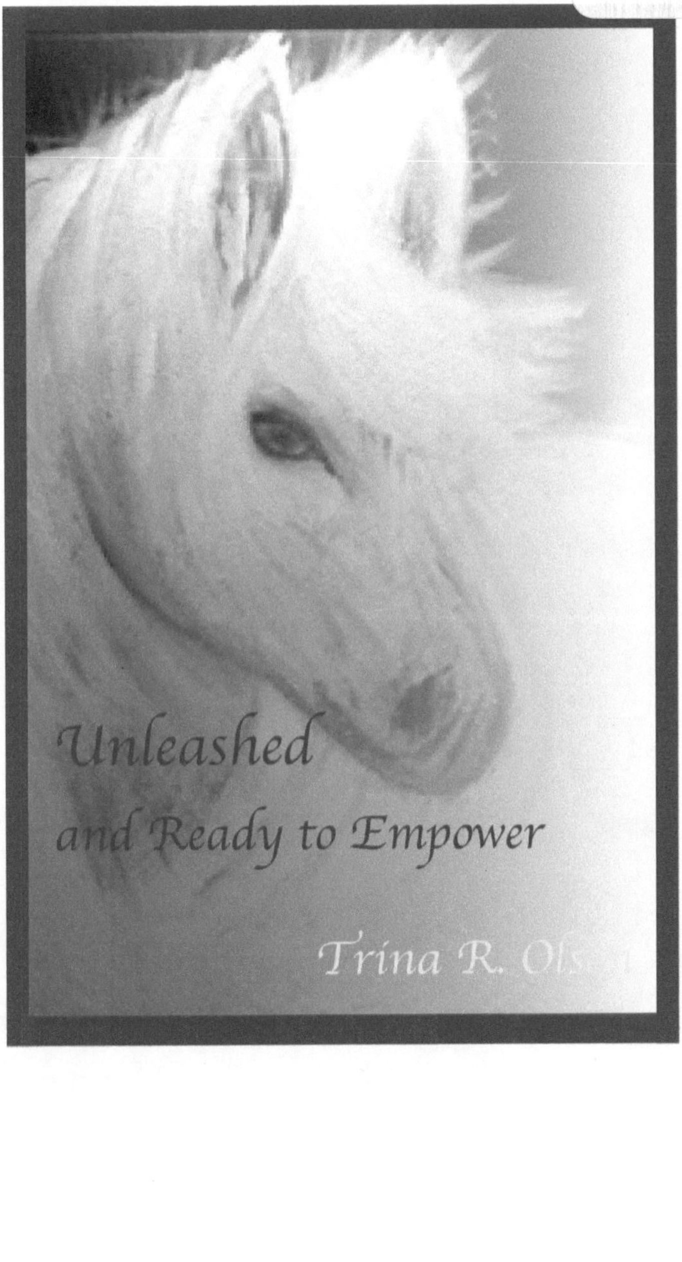

Unleashed
and Ready to Empower

by Trina Rae Olson

© Copyright 2019 – Trina Rae Olson

All rights reserved. This book is protected by the copyright laws of the United States of America. This book may not be copied or reprinted for commercial gain or profit. The use of short quotations or occasional page copying for personal use is permitted and encouraged. Permission will be requested upon request.

Unleashed Publishing, Inc.
975 Wayne Avenue #351
Chambersburg, Pa 17201

We can be reached by calling (717) 860-1848 or through our Website:
unleashedpublishing.net

ISBN-13: 978-1-7333090-1-1
ISBN-10: 1-7333090-1-1

I would like to dedicate this book to my nephew: Mark Olson – your death rocked my world. I felt like my world collapsed when I got the news you were killed in a car accident on March 8, 2008. You see, you didn't know I was asked by God to talk with you six months prior. God wanted me to ask you what your tattoo meant to you. I am sorry, I was scared I would push you away from God. My own life had only just turned around from suicide and I felt I was unable to help anyone else. I am sorry I allowed my own fear to keep me from talking with you that day. At your funeral, a young man stood up and said he had the opportunity to witness to you a few years earlier and you accepted Jesus into your heart. You even had a Bible in the glove box of your car. Were you searching for answers that day when God asked me to speak to you? Questions unanswered!

I am grateful you are in your full glory in Heaven with Father God! Your death helped propel me into the arms of Jesus, giving my life unto God, unto death. I run so hard for Jesus today because I don't want to know that feeling again, when you let God down and miss an opportunity to see someone find the love of Jesus and have an eternal relationship with God the Father, Jesus, and the Holy Spirit.

Mark, I Love you always!

Unleashed and Ready to Empower
Table of Contents

My Life Flashing Before My Eyes	Page 5
The Encounter	Page 8
Purpose, Passion, and Vision	Page 11
Identity Crisis	Page 14
The Journey	Page 29
Empowering a Generation	Page 42
Seeing the Power of God	Page 51
What Does Fear Look Like?	Page 61
Can our Destiny be Delayed or Changed?	Page 78
Can Fear in Your Life Change Your Destiny?	Page 88
God is all About Relationships	Page 115
Claiming our Inheritance	Page 131
Where is the Body of Christ Today?	Page 160
The Difference Between Moses and Pharoah	Page 198
References	Page 214

MY LIFE FLASHING BEFORE MY EYES

And there before me was a door;
a door of life and not death,
a door of purpose and hope and not hopelessness,
a door of being embraced
by a love I never encountered before.

As I saw my car pulled off that embankment,
I saw the hand of God lift me up
through the door that was before me.

The beauty and elegance of life changed me into who I never
knew before! As I looked,
I saw the throne of God; The Father of all Fathers,
the majestic one who called me,
Who knew me before I was conceived,
My Father, as He said "Welcome Home
my beloved daughter".

A warmth covered me and drew me into
His presence erecting a new temple inside of me.

A temple of God that He would now reside in with Jesus in me
where we would be one; one with Jesus who is one with the
Father, that we would be in unity together in this one place that
gives me
free access to the Heavenlies;
Access to my Daddy.

A rainbow of promises encircling the
throne of my heart where God sits seeing Him
tear down lies and restore truth.

As I looked inward into my heart, I saw Heaven.
As I went deeper,

I saw God sitting on the throne of my heart
and the twenty-four elders were enthroned around Him with a
brilliance of white,
calling forth my purity,
calling forth my innocence to once again resound.

Flashes of fire coming from the throne of God
burning away the dross in my heart,
singing away the wounds and sores
to restore it to how it was created,
where my heart was coming to beat with
the heart beat of the Father.

Also before the throne, I saw a sea of glass and the Father
stepping down to ask me to let Him teach me how to dance.

As I learned balance and grace, there was a weaving of wisdom
growing in my strength, a strength from the Father,
a touch of Heaven creating a tapestry of beauty
and elegance in the mantel He placed on my shoulders.

A tender kiss that lured me deep into His heart
further and further.

His eyes were piercing fire
that would go deep into my soul and call forth life.

His hands, gentle and strong to hold His baby girl once again.

THE ENCOUNTER

One night, during worship while on a ministry trip, God took me into a vision. It was intense and full color, like I was right there in the midst of a corral of wild stallions. These stallions were beautiful and majestic. As I was watching intently, I noticed the stallions were all locked in the corral and they were rearing up, trying to break down the fence that was surrounding them. Their nostrils were flared and there was desperation in their squeals.

I very clearly heard these words: "If someone doesn't open the gate soon they are going to get hurt." It broke my heart to see such beautiful stallions being kept locked up when they were meant to be free.

The vision ended and I looked around the large sanctuary. It was full of young adults and youth along with others praising God and worshipping with an extreme passion. I noticed that they were only worshipping from their chairs and would not move out of the area where they were standing. It was like they had passion, but no freedom.

I went back home and really wasn't sure what the encounter meant. A year and a half passed and I found myself heading back to that same country to minister. As I was heading there, God showed me the vision again. This time I saw a hand on the gate, opening the gate. At first I thought it was my hand then I saw the hand of Jesus opening the gate and freeing the stallions.

As I pressed into God, seeking out the meaning of this vision, God said "the stallions are not free to be who they are called to be." I heard God say: "the stallions are captured and their freedom is taken away." They are used as equestrian horses and race horses because of their beauty and elegance.

They are deemed unruly at times and hard to handle. We take away their freedom and expect them to be what we want and wonder why they are unruly. My heart is not to tell anyone they should or shouldn't train and use horses, it is only to share the particular vision that the Lord showed me.

IMPORTANCE
Purpose, Passion, and Vision

God was speaking to me, and asking me to define the purpose of this book and why I feel God wants me to write this book. My heart is to see people find passion in life, to understand their God-given purpose. In spending time with Papa God, they will learn to find vision for their destiny.

To accomplish this, we need to understand our identity in Christ and grasp Who truly lives inside of us. I am still learning more and more every day as I am continually evolving into the person God created me to be here on earth.

My prayers are that as you read this book, you will have greater understanding of who you are and whose you are. Knowing your identity is huge. That knowledge helps destroy the enemy and moves him out of your path as you step through life. It does not mean you will not have tough times, but as you deal with life, you will walk with peace, love, and joy to carry the power and authority of the Kingdom of God into your situations, into your life, into your family, into the lives of your friends, and into the lives of the people you encounter daily.

This book speaks on identity and understanding who Jesus is and what He has done for us to set us free from the chains of the enemy. I believe reading about the revelation God has poured out in my life will help you understand these truths. It is my hope you will also receive your own revelation that will take you deeper into the heart of the Father, building a greater heart connect for you with Papa God, Jesus, and the Holy Spirit.In this book I feel you will see how the scripture comes alive in our daily walk and how we can use the scriptures in life today, making the scriptures also become real and tangible for others.

Part of this book, I feel is to talk about where the Church body is and where it is not, and where it is heading; I feel this is crucial to us walking in our own destiny. We as a Church body need to be in unity, empowering the people to go and be Jesus to the world. We need to be using the gifts God has given us to empower others to be raised up, equipped, and sent out. Jesus was our example, so I pray this book will help you find a greater passion, a greater understanding of your purpose, and find a greater clarity to walk into your destiny, knowing your true identity in Christ. I believe there are people reading this book who once walked out ministry over 40 years ago, but for various reasons lost their fire and the ability to experience the same passion and strength when they ran with God in the beginning. I believe God is giving new dreams and visions and removing the pain of yesterday and catapulting you into an even greater destiny. Everything the enemy comes to steal, kill, and destroy, he has to repay double for our troubles. So get ready to pull out the dreams and visions that were lost, dust them off, and watch God pour out upgrades to those dreams and visions.

IDENTITY CRISIS

I was in the midst of a huge identity crisis in my life when I truly encountered the one, true living God, Jesus Christ. I was finding my identity in everything else in life such as: my illness, my being a screw up in life, and maybe even my inability to be married and in the eyes of the world be successful as a mom and a wife. I really didn't know who I was as God pulled my car off an embankment when I was committing suicide in 2007. I did realize that in the blink of an eye, the person who I had been was gone. As my car came to a stand still suddenly back on the highway, I realized that the person sitting in the car was not the same person I had been just a moment before! I was transformed in a moment. My life was no longer my own and I felt different! I heard God speak these words over me in an audible voice: "You can continue to be stupid, but I (God) have a Plan for your life".

I was freaking out; I didn't know God spoke to anyone, especially me. I had been a Christian in name only for 18 years and never heard anyone tell me God really spoke out loud to anyone. Sometimes I think back to that day and wonder, was I that far away from God that He had to speak audibly so I could hear Him? I don't know if you have ever heard the audible voice of God, but I was undone. In 18 years of "serving" God, I never really knew Him. I knew what Jesus "had done" for my life, but it went no further than that in my life. I didn't really see a change in my life and when I look back, I wonder would I have gone to Heaven in that moment of committing suicide?

I said a few words when I was 20, and yes, I got Baptized and joined the Church. I served in many areas and was diligent to attend Church most Sundays. It was just the thing we were expected to do. I even tried to read the Bible, but it made no sense to me. It never seemed to keep my attention for more than maybe 10 minutes and I surely didn't understand anything I read. Over the years, as I became sicker and sicker, I eventually stopped going to Church because I would just fall asleep. I would go periodically, but not on a regular basis. It just didn't seem to do much for me but interrupt my opportunity to sleep and catch up on some extremely needed rest. I am just being real. When you are sick with everything from Celiac Sprue, Ankylosing Spondylitis, Multiple Sclerosis symptoms, excessive daytime sleepiness, Chronic Fatigue, Fibromyalgia, and so many other issues, rest is the only thing you can do some days. Having to work while being extremely sick is the worst feeling in the world. Up until that point in life, I really only ever heard of what Jesus "had done" for my life and that it was huge. I accepted Him as my Lord and Savior at age 20, but that was the depth of my passion for Him. Since that day in 2007 when God spoke to me, I have been on a journey to go after understanding my identity in Christ and what that means to my life.

Identity- what does that mean to know your identity? Webster's Dictionary definition says that identity is: who someone is and the qualities, beliefs, etc. that make a particular person or group different from others. The Bible says in John 3:16 that "God sent His only begotten son (Jesus) to be our savior and that those who believe in Him will have eternal life". Galatians 3:27-29 says that those who "have been baptized into Christ, have put on Christ". Most people know who Jesus and God are, but a lot of people never seem to come to understand the truth of who God, Jesus, and the Holy Spirit are to us. They never encounter the power and authority of God, nor do they receive the gift of the Spirit that God has instilled in each of us. They also completely miss out in the relationship we were created to have with God, Jesus and the Holy Spirit.

I believed in Jesus and accepted Jesus as my Lord and Savior, then I was baptized and understood that it was a public recognition of my accepting Jesus as my Savior. I believed that if I died, I would go to Heaven and I had a strong faith in that belief. I don't know if I still believe that statement today, and as you read this book you will understand my heart and that this is only my opinion, not Doctrine. God says no one will snatch you out of His hand, but He has given us free will and we have a choice and sometimes I wonder if our choices can cause us to walk out of God's hand? I went for 18 years as a Christian, believing in Jesus and knowing about who God was, but I wasn't able to comprehend what it really meant. When I would try to read the Bible, I would just get frustrated and bored. I would get nothing out of reading the Bible.

What was missing? Why did I struggle to know the One who I knew saved me and gave me eternal life? What do you do next to understand the MORE that I was missing in my life?

What was missing was the Baptism of the Holy Spirit which empowers you with inner strength through His Spirit. Ephesians 3:16 tells us, "I pray that from His glorious, unlimited resources He will empower you with inner strength through His Spirit." Jesus said He needed "to leave so that the Comforter would be able to come to abide in you forever". John 14:16 says "And I will pray the Father, and He shall give you another Comforter, that He may abide with you forever." John 16:7 also talks about the Comforter. In John 20:21, Jesus breathed on them so they would receive the Holy Ghost. John 20:21-22 says, "Then said Jesus to them again, Peace be unto you: as my Father hath sent me, even so send I you. And when he had said this, he breathed on them, and saith unto them, Receive ye the Holy Ghost".

They already believed in Jesus and had walked with Him for over three years. It was not about saying a prayer for them to be instantly overcome by the Spirit of God. I believe there is no rhyme or reason as to how each of us receives the Holy Spirit. I do know that throughout the entire Book of Acts, there are many times people received the Baptism of the Holy Spirit before the Water Baptism. There are also times it happened after the Water Baptism and there are times it all happened at the same time. I believe with Paul it happened at the encounter when he was knocked off his horse and encountered Jesus. In Acts 10: 44-48, it speaks of the entire group of Gentiles starting to speak in tongues as the Holy Spirit fell upon their group while Peter was speaking about the free gift of Jesus. He proclaimed that anyone who believed would receive forgiveness of sins through the name of Jesus.

In these scriptures it is also asked if anyone could forbid or refuse water for Baptizing these people, seeing that they had received the Holy Spirit just as the disciples had. This is an incredible encounter where the Holy Spirit crashed in on an entire group and it was not about praying a prayer. It was through a heart connect with God.

It was not all about a select group of people either, because Philip was called by the Angel of the Lord to go to the desert road to meet the Ethiopian eunuch. During this meeting, Philip listened to the voice of God. He went over to the chariot and heard the man reading in the Book of Isaiah. Wow, what an incredible, divine encounter which helped explain to the eunuch what he was reading. It also opened a door for Philip to speak to him about Jesus. As they went by some water, the Ethiopian eunuch asked if he could be Baptized and Philip Baptized him and the Spirit of the Lord then took Philip away and the eunuch went on his way, rejoicing.

Acts 3:19 talks about repentance as an actual turn around, to return to God. God will erase your sins and a time of refreshing comes from the presence of the Lord. I believe you will see a complete change in a person when they accept Jesus as their Lord and Savior. In Acts 19:2-7, Paul came upon 12 disciples in Ephesus and asked them a question that baffled me when I first read it in scriptures: "Did you receive the Holy Spirit when you believed?" Wow! I was undone! Paul asks this approximately 10-15 years after Jesus was crucified; this was Paul, not the first 12 Apostles, and he saw that these people were Disciples. Their response blew my mind: "No, we have not even heard that there is a Holy Spirit." I could understand this if they were just regular people who have not been reached yet, but they were Disciples! They had been Baptized in the Baptism of Repentance, of John and when Paul laid hands on them, they were Baptized in the Holy Spirit and something extraordinary happened. The Holy Spirit came upon them and they spoke in tongues and prophesied!

What if the Church had already started to take shape outside of the heart of God just a short 10-15 years after Jesus was crucified? Yes, they could have been doing good, but how much can we do for God? When we truly receive the Baptism of the Holy Spirit, there is a transformation in our lives. The day God turned my life around, I was filled with the Holy Spirit and the proof started to manifest in my life a few weeks later when I started to read the Bible and couldn't put it down! I had never read more than two books in my life prior to my encounter and now I didn't want to do anything but read the Bible! I couldn't get enough of the revelation God was pouring out to me through the Holy Spirit.

I feel in my heart that I was filled with the Holy Spirit the day God pulled my car off that embankment when I was committing suicide. As the hand of God pulled my car off the embankment, I know I experienced a change in my heart. God caused my car to stop, and turned it heading the opposite direction, showing me that my life was just turned around prophetically. He spoke to me that day in an audible voice which was a total shock! I don't feel anyone really knew how to explain to me about God really talking to someone. God told me that day that I "could continue to be stupid", but He "had a plan for my life!" I consider that day to be the beginning of the rest of my life. I had prayed a prayer a long time before that day, but was there ever really a heart connect with God? Or was I the prodigal one who God was still waiting for to return?

I do know that my life has truly been transformed since that day and I totally give credit to all those who prayed for me. I believe our prayers are very powerful; those prayers caused God's hand to pull my car off that embankment as my car was starting to flip. I believe years of prayers came into action that very day.

The bowl of prayers tipped that very day into an overflow of Love of the Father pouring into my car that hot summer day. I felt an incredible peace fall over me that day and an intense change happened within my life. I now dealt with life like I never could have before those moments. It was as if my brokenness was washed away and my pain and wounds disappeared in an instant. I was truly changed in a moment.

The main difference between since this encounter with God in 2007 is that I now have an incredibly intimate relationship with God, Jesus, and the Holy Spirit. I had been a Christian for 18 years and had never once encountered anything like I have experienced over these incredible years since that day in 2007. I know that my biggest goal now is to seek the Kingdom of God, knowing that all else will follow, falling into place. It is not about anything else, only God.

As I seek Him, I will hear the Plans He has for me and the connection between my heart's desires and God's Will for my life come into alignment and then begin coming to fruition. I want it to be known someday that "they knew she had been in the presence of Jesus".

My heart is to see other people encounter God, knowing that it looks different for each person. I don't feel we can put a formula together that will always work, nor is it simply about a specific prayer to pray to transform us. I am not saying that a person can't be changed by a praying a prayer, but we can't expect that to work for each person. David Wilkerson from Teen Challenge speaks about the difference of people set free from drug and alcohol addiction who could go back into the very place they came out of without falling into the same habits of their past. He said there was one thing that was common to all of them: the infilling of the Holy Spirit empowered them to stand against who they were in the past, knowing that they were not the same person as before. They understood they now had Jesus living inside of them and they carried the power and authority of God Almighty with them everywhere they went.

Instead of having someone pray a prayer, what if we pray with them asking the Holy Spirit to Baptize them in the Holy Spirit, guiding them and filling them completely, then in the midst of the prayer having them repent and to accept Jesus as Lord of their life. Taking time to pray is the beginning, and then stay connected with that person to help them walk out their conversion. We all need to be discipled because God is about relationship. It is through a relationship that doors open for us to speak life into others. Relationships are what the Bible is all about: Elijah walked beside Elisha; Samuel and Jonathan walked beside David; Paul walked beside Timothy. However, there are times when we are called to walk out our Destiny with no specific person beside us. It is necessary to ask the Father about this and important to know the different seasons we are in.

Is it a once and done, one-time infilling? Scripture speaks of continually being filled. I also believe that this is not a one-time infilling with the Holy Spirit. Scripture says we should be continually filled and stimulated with the Holy Spirit! Ephesians 5:18 says "And do not get drunk with wine, for that is debauchery; but ever be filled and stimulated with the Holy Spirit." (The Amplified Bible)

THE JOURNEY
Understanding Your Identity in Christ

I believe Jesus was sent here to be an example for us to follow and we can't follow someone who is not tangible to us. I have been praying about this. I feel God keeps showing me more about my identity as I continue to get revelation from God.

This journey allowed something to really snap inside to help me understand more of my identity in Christ. During a Church service a few years ago, the speaker spoke on Luke 3, the Baptism of Jesus. I can't explain what happened, but God started to really touch my heart in a deeper way that day.

Luke 3:21-22

"When all the people were being baptized, Jesus was baptized too. And as He was praying, heaven was opened and the Holy Spirit descended on Him in bodily form like a dove. And a voice came from heaven: "You are my Son, whom I love; with you I am well pleased."

When I heard the words as I was reading it in my Bible, God grabbed my heart and I felt a shift in my spirit like I had never felt before. Those words changed my life: "the Holy Spirit descended on Him in bodily form like a dove." God Himself descended upon Jesus. God Almighty came down and went in to Jesus. The person of the Holy Spirit lived inside of Him from that point onward! Wow, I had read this many times but never saw that it was in "bodily form"! Was Jesus the same as you and I before the Holy Spirit descended upon Him? Did the same Holy Spirit of God come into us at our baptism as came inside of Jesus at His baptism?

Jesus was then tempted in the wilderness for 40 days afterward, but He didn't go there until He was filled with the Spirit of God. While in the wilderness, the angels of the Lord protected Jesus! This is just like God has his angels interact within our lives. Questions started really stirring my heart to understand more of what God was beginning to show me. Over the next few months, I prayed for God to show me His heart. I wanted to know what He was saying, not what commentaries or other people said. I wanted to hear straight from God.

My search grew deeper, trying to know who truly lived inside of me. God was taking me on an incredible journey that has been full of His revelation. Without a doubt I know the Holy Spirit was showing me the revelation of the living God, Jesus Christ living inside of me. Yes, my mind knew this, but there was a greater understanding of this needed in my heart. As I continued on a path to set my mind on the things above, and not on earthly things, Colossians 3:1-4 started to really speak to me.

Colossians 3:1-4

"Since, then you have been raised with Christ, set your hearts on things above, where Christ is seated at the right hand of God. Set your minds on things above, not on earthly things. For you died, and your life is now hidden with Christ in God. When Christ who is your life, appears, then you also will appear with him in glory."

So my search and prayers became set upon asking God to show me more and to help me understand who I really was. Who really resides inside of my heart? I didn't have the time to sit down and search out the scriptures. I felt peace about God showing me the connections and the scriptures. The next place God took me into the scriptures was John 17 which is the last prayer Jesus prayed recorded in the Bible.

Jesus Prays to Be Glorified:

After Jesus said this, He looked toward heaven and prayed:

"Father, the hour has come. Glorify your Son, that your Son may glorify you.² For you granted Him authority over all people that He might give eternal life to all those you have given Him.³ Now this is eternal life: that they know you, the only true God, and Jesus Christ, whom you have sent.⁴ I have brought you glory on earth by finishing the work you gave me to do.⁵ And now, Father, glorify me in your presence with the glory I had with you before the world began."

Jesus was saying He brought glory to God while on earth by finishing the work God gave Him to do. Wow! That is how we can give Glory to God, by finishing the work He gives us to do. Now the question is: how to know what this is in my life?

Jesus Prays for His Disciples:

[6] *"I have revealed you, to those whom you gave me out of the world. They were yours; you gave them to me and they have obeyed your word.* [7] *Now they know that everything you have given me comes from you.* [8] *For I gave them the words you gave me and they accepted them. They knew with certainty that I came from you, and they believed that you sent me.* [9] *I pray for them. I am not praying for the world, but for those you have given me, for they are yours.* [10] *All I have is yours, and all you have is mine. And glory has come to me through them.* [11] *I will remain in the world no longer, but they are still in the world, and I am coming to you. Holy Father, protect them by the power of your name, the name you gave me, so that they may be one as we are one.* [12] *While I was with them, I protected them and kept them safe by that name you gave me. None has been lost except the one doomed to destruction so that Scripture would be fulfilled."*

Jesus's glory comes to Him through the ones God gave Him (us). Jesus protected them while He was with them. Jesus was going to the Father and He was asking God the Father to protect us by the power of the name God gave Jesus. Jesus was asking God the Father for us all to be one with Him, and God, the Father. His name has power and protection.

We see that today when we are in trouble, we can call upon His name, Jesus. The enemy submits only to the name of Jesus; what power and authority are found within that name!

[13] "I am coming to you now, but I say these things while I am still in the world, so that they may have the full measure of my joy within them. [14] I have given them your word and the world has hated them, for they are not of the world any more than I am of the world. [15] My prayer is not that you take them out of the world but that you protect them from the evil one. [16] They are not of the world, even as I am not of it. [17] Sanctify them by the truth; your word is truth. [18] As you sent me into the world, I have sent them into the world. [19] For them I sanctify myself, that they too may be truly sanctified."

Jesus' prayer is asking for us to have **the full measure of His joy** within us! The full measure of His joy! Is this the overflowing infilling of the Holy Spirit? He doesn't say we will be loved by the world, but that the world will hate us! He asks the Father not to take us out of the world, but to protect us from the evil one. Not to take us out of our problems, nor out of our situations, but to protect us. Maybe to protect us as we go through the stuff in our lives, helping us to gain character and confidence as we overcome those problems and situations. People are waiting on God to snatch them out of their problems, and that is not Jesus' prayer for us!

He prayed that we would be sanctified by the truth; God's word is the truth! Sanctify in the Greek means to separate from profane things and dedicate to God. Jesus also said that just as God sent Him into the world, He was also sending us into the world. Jesus sanctified Himself that we may also be sanctified by Him.

What does it look like to be sanctified in our lives? Giving it all to God and holding nothing back. What does that look like in your life? I feel that it is like Peter standing on the boat, realizing that he had denied Jesus three times and suddenly he knew he had a chance to walk with

Jesus one more time, giving his life fully and unfiltered, giving of his life to Jesus unto death, unto the cross. John 21 is a perfect example of what Peter was dealing with when he saw Jesus standing on the beach. Yes, John had to help Peter see that it was Jesus on the shore! Wow, even in that, are you like John helping someone else to see what is standing not too far off in their life?

Peter had Jesus breathe on him in John 20 and Jesus said "receive the Holy Spirit". Yet they had just gone back to what they knew, fishing on the right side and while they were doing what they knew to do, Jesus met them in that moment of their lives. Peter grabbed his outer garment which he had taken off. What if that "outer garment" was taken off when he denied Jesus three times? Maybe it is more spiritual than we think - what if "outer garment" represents the identity of Christ that Peter took off when he denied Jesus before Jesus went to the Cross? Grabbing an upgrade and laying down everything, I believe Peter dove into the things of God that day not looking back and carrying all those fish to Jesus without losing even one. What if that net and those fish were prophetic to his life - that he was not going to lose even one person he would go after for God and that the net would not tear for any to get away or be hurt in the process? Peter was sold out to Jesus in that moment for life! Undone, he knew the cost of not having Jesus and he was not going to walk away from Him again. Peter gave everything unto the Lord, unto death, and even unto the Cross.

So what do you think? Do you think that is a true understanding of sanctification? I believe most people don't even have that word in their vocabulary. If that is a true example of sanctification, how many Christians do you know, or are you yourself even willing to truly lay your life down for Jesus even if it was unto death? I am not talking about being a martyr. I am talking about giving everything to the Lord and trusting God above everyone and everything in your life! I saw my life transform in front of me, as I had been a Christian for 18 years but only knew of God and Jesus. As my car came off that embankment in July of 2007, everything changed in my life and who I was a moment before was not who I was becoming. Yes, I really can't even understand who I really was before God transformed my life.

Do I have everything together? No, I am still a work in progress, but one thing I do know is that each day I pray I am one step closer to who God created me to be! Where are you in your journey? If you have everything together, you might be standing at the pearly gates! I pray this book takes you deeper into the things of God and helps you to find a greater understanding of who you are in Christ! I pray that through this book you will see yourself grow into a closer walk with Jesus and a greater understanding of the the person God has created you to be also. I pray that as you read this book, you find yourself Unleashed and Ready to Empower others!

Empowering A Generation

In order to build faith and confidence within your spiritual walk with the Lord, there are some key questions to ask of the Father:

- Who is your spiritual family?
- Who is lifting you up to God like Moses did for Joshua?
- Who is lifting up your arms like Aaron and Hur?
- Who is your Caleb or has God used you like Caleb to come alongside of a Joshua?
- Who is like a Joshua that you are lifting up to God?
- How are you directing others to God?

Keeping accountability in your life and holding others accountable is crucial to staying humble, righteous, and wholly set apart unto the Lord God Almighty. We also need to help others build faith, confidence, and boldness to help them follow after the heart of God.

The battle of Amalek in the Bible, I feel, is an example which shows is pertinent to our lives. In this battle, God uses unity to bring victory over the Amalek in Exodus 17. It takes unity and working together to see the enemy defeated so that the Israelites can move forward into the next season of their walk.

The victory took Moses, Aaron, Hur, Joshua, and Caleb, along with a select army working together as they went into the battle against the Amalek. Moses delegated authority to Joshua to select men to go to battle. We need to believe in others enough to lift them up and empower them to go after the enemy at hand and win the battle that before them. Those who have walked beside you in other battles are sometimes the very ones God is asking you to lift up and to trust so that they can be used by God to win the next battle.

God didn't allow Joshua to win the battle with the Amalek without the other four people. I would like to use this battle in Exodus 17 to show you how this applies to our own lives and how it is important to be lifted up by others and to lift others up in our lives, while also holding each other accountable. As we walk through each battle in our lives, we need to continue to have our eyes on Jesus and not on the battle, the victory, or each other. This is critical to the victory!

Let your self imagination visualize yourself in this battle in Exodus 17:9-14. You have Moses as your spiritual father and he has the Rod of God which carries the Power and Authority of God and he is trying with all his might to keep holding up the Rod of God while Joshua has the Sword of God to fight. While Moses keeps his arms up, Joshua and the army gain victory but as soon as his arms drop, the Amalek army begins to gain victory: "and it came to pass, when Moses held up his hand, that Israel prevailed: and when he let down his hand, Amalek prevailed." Exodus 17:11

What does that look like in our lives? I believe we need people in our lives to speak life into us and the church as a whole has fallen short in this area. We don't see spiritual mothers and fathers lifting up their sons and daughters. We don't see them encouraging them to go into battle and we rarely see them supported financially to help them through the battle as they go into the mission field of America or the Nations abroad. We see others encourage us to raise support and to work to earn the money to go into the mission field, but where is the Body of Christ to lift those called to go up to go?

We see people lifting others up spiritually through prayer, but how many people do you hear of who are truly willing to stand on the hill praying while the main battles are being waged? We as the church body have entered into lack in spiritual, emotional, physical, and financial areas even though we wish to lift up those sons and daughters we send out to be in the midst of the darkest of dark battles against the enemy. When we go into a battle against the enemy, we always need people to be lifting us up through intercession that carries the authority and power to declare victory. We cannot win any of these battles on our own!

Imagine yourself in each of these different people's shoes right in the heart of the battle in Exodus 17. Imagine you are on the front line in charge of all the soldiers that you hand-selected and you have the responsibility to see victory without losing any lives in the battle. What does that look like today in our own lives? One example could be that you have served under another Pastor or Apostle and now the reigns are being handed over to you to run with. Can you find the vision that was originally set forth in the ministry, business, or organization? If not the same vision, do you have a clear vision and people that will encourage you to walk it out? You will have new territory to claim and God says everywhere you place the sole of your feet, you claim territory (Deut. 11:24). Do you believe in your vision to the degree that you can explain it to others to incorporate backing to encourage and sustain you as you walk this out in faith? Joshua and Caleb had a Spirit of God upon them that was different than the others and they stood out among the rest. The important part of their walk was that they had faith and trusted God, being sold out and passionate to persevere and finish their journey with God no matter the opposition!

Can you walk as a Caleb if God has called you to walk alongside of a Joshua? Could you walk beside someone God is lifting up to be a leader to help lift him/her up and to help them stay accountable? Can you help someone else who is put in the leadership role by God even when you are doing just as much work? Can you walk this walk believing for decades that some day God will open the door for you to also claim your territory that was promised to you, knowing you are just as strong as you once were when you first heard? Can you hang onto a promise until you see the timing and season for you to step into that promise and stay close to God the whole time so that you carry His strength into the promise to claim victory?

Can you be the voice for a Moses and stay humble to lift him up in order to help others and to understand your purpose in life while seeing the vision God has given someone else?

The main thing is to seek out God and through your relationship with Papa God, Jesus, and Holy Spirit you will see vision, purpose, and passion to run with God with all your heart sold out to Him! I would like to propose to those who have been struggling to find that Moses in your life, that maybe all the ones called as a Moses to come alongside you have not yet stepped into their proper position, or maybe there are those who tried but were not strong enough to walk it out as God was calling them to.

I believe there are many people called who are struggling to know how to begin to walk it all out. I believe they are finding their way through the guidance of the Holy Spirit. I believe that this generation has a different Spirit about them that empowers them to persevere. Moses was following after God, but God said that Joshua and Caleb had a different Spirit about them in the sense that it allowed them to have their eyes open to see things differently than previous generations.

Seeing the Power of God
God Removed the Confidence and Courage from the People of Jericho!

Picture this scene from the walls of Jericho: they were a powerful group of people who were full of confidence and courage. The Israelites believed they were giants from the reports of their ten spies. The story gets to the people of Jericho about how the Power of the God of Israel opened the up the Red Sea for them to cross, yet as the Egyptians went after them, the Egyptians were all killed by the huge waves. Hearing that all the Israelites crossed over the Red Sea safely on dry ground but not one of the Egyptians made it out alive caused the people of Jericho to pay attention. Put yourself in the sandals of the people of Jericho, what would you think about this group of people who miraculously crossed over safely while the powerful Egyptians all perished? Do you think you would cower in a corner with fear? Can you imagine as the report got back to Joshua and Caleb what they thought? Confidence in Joshua and Caleb had to go through the roof for them to believe God was about to do it again!

What would that do to you? Rahab told Joshua that God removed all the confidence and courage from the people of Jericho. Wow! If you didn't know God and if He wasn't with you, that would set a fear inside of you that would destroy you! They saw the power of this almighty God and if Moses would have simply trusted in the report from Joshua and Caleb and found a way to bring peace to the Israelites, they would have conquered Jericho 40 years earlier than they actually did.

I don't believe the Israelites were ready; God removed the Israelites from Egypt, but now He needed to remove the Egyptian and slave mentality from the Israelites. Their rebellion and complaining caused all of them to die in the desert over the 40 years they spent wandering in the wilderness. It was the next generation that God used to take to the promise land, and I believe God needed a generation that would move in unity, a generation who didn't have the slave mentality blocking them from claiming their inheritance. He was raising up a generation who saw themselves as conquerors, not grasshoppers, and who would be led by Joshua and Caleb who saw themselves differently as well. Joshua and Caleb knew their God and had faith in what He would do for them and through them.

This new generation would not be able to tangibly understand what slavery looked like for they were raised as warriors. A slave will love their Master out of fear or respect, but has no relationship with their Master. God wants relationship and is raising up a generation of Sons and Daughters to claim their heritage.

God says He goes before us and after us and will gird us up in the midst. The cloud went before the Israelites to guide them during the day and the fire went behind them at night. "By day the LORD went ahead of them in a pillar of cloud to guide them on their way and by night in a pillar of fire to give them light, so that they could travel by day or night." (Exodus 13:21) God protected them in the midst. He provided for their every need, even their clothes and shoes never wore out. For 40 years God provided all they needed while they wandered in the wilderness.

The report of Rahab to the spies confirmed what Joshua and Caleb saw 40 years earlier when they went in to Jericho to spy out the land. They saw themselves as conquerors while the other ten saw themselves as grasshoppers. They rose up against Caleb when he went to make a stand. The Israelites just didn't know any other way; they where gripped with fear, they had been continually put down as slaves and still carried the same slave mentality into the desert. Sometimes we struggle to get rid of our old mindset. How would you react if you had only known slavery all your life? Would you be able to look past the seen, into the unseen realm and be able to believe for the unseen? Where in your life have you seen something similar in today's society? Maybe, when you approach someone who has never known that God could heal? Maybe even when you try to tell some people they have value and worth? Our culture has gone so far away from identity in Christ and knowing that the gifts described and testified to in the Bible are for today. It is so far beyond anything people can comprehend that sometimes when they see it, they still don't understand that God can do that through them and even more, that He wants to do those things with them in relationship with Him!

Joshua 2:8-11

"Before the spies lay down for the night, she went up on the roof and said to them, "I know that the Lord has given you this land and that a great fear of you has fallen on us, so that all who live in this country are melting in fear because of you. We have heard how the Lord dried up the water of the Red Sea for you when you came out of Egypt and what you did to Sihon and Og, the two kings of the Amorites east of the Jordan, whom you completely destroyed. **When we heard of it, our hearts melted in fear and everyone's courage failed because of you, for the Lord your God is God in heaven above and on the earth below."**

Rahab saw something different also! I believe this story helps us understand that with God, all things are possible even when you are going into the land of the giants. God will also fight the battle that He calls you to into. The walls fell, not because of the power of the men, but because of the power and authority of God to change and shift atmospheres. Father God said He will make the mountains in front of you be cast into the sea by the words that are in your mouth!

He gives us such a power and authority when we walk with Him. He wants relationship; He wants communion with us. He is a Father that wants to get to know His Beloved Sons and Daughters.

Make time to spend with the Father. Sit down with a piece of paper today and ask Him the questions you want answered. Talk to Him and let Him talk to you. The more you do this, the more you will learn and understand how to hear from Papa God.

I believe we are also created to have relationships with Jesus and the Holy Spirit because they are all one, yet they function in different ways. There will be different times when you will interact with Jesus and the Holy Spirit, just as you do with God. They reside inside of you so it is important to start tapping into your heart more so you will know the fullness of what is now living inside of you. Let the junk from the world be removed and be replaced with more of the Love of the Father. Let the joy of Jesus continue to enrapture you and allow yourself to be guided by the Spirit.

It is important to continue to have friends who are spirit-led Christians speaking into your life and holding you accountable. Learning to discern the voice you hear is easier when you can talk to someone else to know when you are hearing from God, from yourself, from the enemy or even hearing the voice of others.

Don't be afraid. Begin to pray to the Father unceasingly, asking Him to show you how to do this. Ask Him to take you to scripture that shows you who you are and how much He loves you. Let the scriptures bring revelation straight from God to you, helping you to learn your identity more and more every day.

God told Moses to create a book of remembrance for Joshua, to remind him who he was. God had Joshua put stones at the other side of the Jordan to remind the Israelites of what God did for them and to help prevent them from going back to where they had been mentally.

Renewing your mind daily, I believe, is simply knowing your identity in Christ and meditating on the Word of God to reaffirm His love for you. Position yourself with a positive mindset and know that everything that the enemy throws your way is nothing and cannot hurt you or your future. You have control over how much the enemy can hurt you. You choose: life or death? You choose: overcoming or retreat? You choose your path and God will go along for the ride! He is not about control and He won't force His will on us! Choose to step into a greater relationship every day with Father God, Jesus, and the Holy Spirit!

Time of Reflection (Fear or Faith)

What has God been talking to you about while reading about fear and how it affects us in our lives?

Ask God to show you any areas of fear in your life that are keeping you from walking where He is calling you!

- Have you ever spoken out about not allowing God to do something in your life and felt fear grip you when you even thought about walking into an area God has put on your heart?
- This may be a time to repent, because that is making a vow and God won't force us to do anything!
- Have you ever doubted being able to do something because it looks too huge for you to do it? Maybe it is too large for you, but not for God to do!
- If it is huge, it usually is God, because it is beyond our ability and we will need to lean on God.

What Does Fear Look Like?

What does fear look like? Where is fear lurking in our lives? How can we close the door of fear so it no has longer a hold on us? Can fear keep us from doing the will of God?

These are some questions touching my heart since March of 2008. This testimony actually began in September of 2007, only 3 months after God pulled my car out of the hands of the enemy. I had fallen into a deep depression inside my heart that was killing me. God took me from the brink of death that day on July 5, 2007 and started me on a path that forever changed my life.

I was driving to Philadelphia for work one September day and felt that God was talking to me about speaking to my nephew, Mark. At that time, Mark was about 23. Mark had dreams of playing professional baseball and a heart of gold, but he never saw his big break through a door opening for him to play for the pros. One of the greatest characteristics about Mark was his love for people. He would always befriend the unloved person. He loved hard and friendships meant a lot to him.

As I thought about Mark, I sensed God asking me to speak to him about the tattoo of a cross he had recently gotten on his right bicep. That stirred me up. At this point I was still trying to find my way in life dealing with all the recent changes since God pulled my car off of the embankment as I was committing suicide. I wondered how I would speak to Mark about the cross? Wow - that made me sweat and cry at the same time! You see, I didn't feel worthy to be used by God and, even though the depression was broken off my life, I still had fear of rejection. Insecurity and unworthiness plagued my mind and gripped my heart. What if he said NO? What if he rejected me because I was "preaching to him"? The "What if" questions just started to eat away at any faith I had to be used by God to touch someone else's life.

The memories of my own High School years came flooding back, with my own responses to Christian friends who desperately tried to reach my heart for God. I would put my hand up and say, "Talk to the hand". I was not interested in hearing who this God was or wasn't. I had so much pain in my heart as a teenager that the pain was overwhelming me and causing me to slowly suffocate from heartbreak. I remember my Mom occasionally taking me to Church and my sister trying to get me and her two sons to go to Church. It only worked for short periods of time.

Therefore, I knew about this man, Jesus, but really was not interested at that time. My heart was wondering, "if there is a God, why did he let my family lose so many loved ones in such a short period of time?"

The Olson family was an incredible, happy-go-lucky family, full of love and we touched the hearts of many friends. I grew up in a house of love, or love to the degree we knew what love looked like. The friends of my brothers and sisters came to our house like it was their own, at any hour of the night. Then things started to change.

I was 14 years old when we get a knock on the door in the wee hours of the morning. My older sister, Sherry, who was living with us at that time had been killed in a one car accident. The driver was driving drunk and had lost control of the vehicle and the car had flipped into a concrete culvert along a main road on the mountain. She had two beautiful daughters who were my age. Now my sister, who was my best friend, was not in our lives any longer which slung me into a whirlwind of a downward spiral even in school. At that time, schools didn't really look into helping students going through a tragedy and I don't remember anyone reaching out to me.

Just 11 months later, we get another shocking visit as my brother and I were pulling into the High School parking lot. My aunt was waiting for the bus to arrive to take my brother to the hospital because my Dad had been in an accident at work and he was in a coma. I was sent to my grandparents. He lived for five days in a coma before he died. It did give us a chance to say good-bye, but it was really tough.

Then, right as I graduated from High School, we received another horrific phone call while on vacation. My 4-year-old niece was riding in the back seat of my sister-in-law's (her mom) car and they were hit by a drunk driver. Bethy had no chance and died instantly. She was a precious joy to our entire family and I loved her with all my heart. One of the worst times of my life was to have her taken from us in such a senseless way.

How much more can a family take? I think that for years, I waited for the next person to leave without notice. It haunted me for so many years; who would be next?

I shared all that to set the tone for what I was feeling inside as I was struggling inside over talking to Mark. In those years, I knew deep pain that kept me from wanting to know God, because I blamed God for taking my family members one by one. I didn't want any part of a God that would allow so much to happen to one family. I just didn't understand who God was and judged Him without knowing or experiencing His great love for us.

I was just coming to understand the love of God and that there was so much more to know about him. When He asked me to talk to Mark about his tattoo. I was learning God is awesome. He even opened a door and gave me an opportunity to hang out with Mark all by ourselves one day. Mark had a muscle tee-shirt on and the tattoo was visible. Fear gripped my heart and I allowed my faith in the enemy (fear) to be greater than my faith in God! I have no doubt Mark would have told me about his tattoo as I look back on that opportunity. I knew Mark's heart; he would have talked to me and told me what it meant to him. It would have opened the door to talk about God, but I chose to allow fear to divert my conversation in another direction that day.

Six months later, I was awakened by God at about 11:30–12:00 midnight. He did this many nights. Since I didn't have to work the next day, I just dove into prayer and reading the Bible. I don't remember what I was reading, but I now know God was preparing my heart for what was happening. I got a phone call from my brother at about 3 AM, because he saw the light on in my bedroom as he sat in our driveway. I told him God had woken me up at about midnight and that I was reading my Bible and spending time with God, praying. He asked me to open the door and then the news fell from his mouth. Mark was pinned in his Suburban that was wrapped around a telephone pole and he had been dead several for hours.

Not again I thought, he was so young! Our Marky was dead! No! No! I was so broken inside. I wasn't even sure where Mark was with God. Had I missed the one opportunity for him to hear about God? I don't know what Abraham felt when he didn't obey God and pursued his own solution by having Ishmael, but I do know that I felt like I let both Mark and God down! Did Mark know God? My heart was broken and gripped with so much pain. I vowed that day that I wanted to be used by God and I prayed that I would never walk in disobedience ever again. I prayed I would never feel that kind of pain again.

Mark was pinned for over five hours in the vehicle as the emergency crews worked hard to set another pole in place in order to move the transformer that was resting on his body. I'm not sure about all the details, but I wondered why they couldn't just move the pole and brace it somewhere else. The highway was shut down for quite some time and it seemed like the nightmare would never end. It was a Freak accident, yet another young Olson's life was taken far too soon, and far too quick without any chance to say good-bye!

At the funeral, a young man stood up and said that he had a chance to lead Mark to Christ a few years earlier. When I heard those words, I about passed out from relief. I was so excited because I knew Mark knew God! I never really mourned the loss of his life much after that day, because I was starting to look at death differently. I now knew it was not an end, but a new beginning to the rest of eternal life with Christ. Mark was in an awesome place with Jesus!

In those early days of my walk, I believe fear cost me something very valuable. A little while after Mark's death, my brother (Mark's Dad) told me Mark had a Bible in his car and that he also wore a gold cross around his neck. Was God prompting me so I could both learn more about God? What an opportunity, as a young Christian, to have my family walk this out with me. Was Mark in the same place I was 18 years earlier, just needing some help to understand the Bible? If I would have talked with Mark, would he be alive today? Questions that I wanted to know the answers to, but I also know that I cannot live in regret! I know that God is amazing and gentle and kind, and He gave me a safe place to start my Christian walk. Yet the enemy still stole from our family; Mark would have been such a great evangelist who loved the unloved and had a heart of gold.

Mark's death was not in vain. I know God didn't cause the accident and that He was with him through those last moments. I have allowed God to use Mark's death to catapult me even deeper into ministry while being held deeply in the arms of the Father. That one moment in my life has impacted me beyond words. I pray reading this also impacts your life to the degree that you will not allow fear to keep you from walking in obedience to God. Obedience is so crucial to our walk and our relationship with God. Joyce Meyers says it this way, "if you can't get rid of the fear to do what you are called to do, then you do it with the fear and that will put the enemy under your feet." Great advice!

Life is not about living in regret of the past, rather it is about leaning into the heart of Jesus and finding the lessons of those moments to propel you into a greater walk in your Destiny with Father God. Are there places in your life where you feel you royally screwed up? Scripture says in Genesis 50:20, "You intended to harm me, but God intended it for good to accomplish what is now being done, the saving of many lives." In this scripture, Joseph was talking to his brothers and he was helping them to understand to not be afraid, that he had forgiven them. Like Joseph, many of us have been hurt by others. No matter if it was intentional or accidental, lives are impacted whether for good or bad, and every action has a reaction. What we do with those moments in our lives is what makes the difference. How we react to those moments is the key to what love looks like! Joseph chose to look beyond the pain and hurt and kept his eyes on God. It doesn't mean he did everything right all the time, but it is the position of the heart that God is looking at in the end. Joseph didn't retaliate toward his brothers, instead he was a solution to his brothers' future struggles for food. Joseph was the door to help them; through him they found life.

Is there someone you hurt but you won't cross the line to hand them an olive branch for fear they will react in the same way you treated them, no matter if it was intentional or accidental? Joseph walked with God and it was only through God that he had the strength to endure the tragic events in his life. God can help you overcome those moments that grip your life also.

Are you willing to look past someone else's shortcomings in life to give them another chance? Are you willing to lay down your fear of reaping the consequences by asking someone to forgive you of a wrong you have done? In all of these questions, I am praying you seek out the Kingdom of God and watch God move in those areas of your life. We have ALL fallen short in life and we have ALL been a pawn in the enemy's game to steal, kill, or destroy parts of other people's lives, no matter whether it was intentional or accidental. Grace covers all!

It is time to stop letting fear grip you! Fear is actually faith in the enemy! Our God is bigger than any mountain in front of our lives. Take a look at your life and ask God to reveal through the Holy Spirit if there are any areas that prevent you from walking out your Destiny or even just walking in complete obedience to God? As God reveals those moments, without going and digging up something that is not there, just give them to Jesus. One way to do this is to close your eyes and visualize Jesus standing before you. As you visualize Jesus, hand over that situation or person to Jesus and if you were in the wrong, recognize it and repent of the wrong doing and ask the Holy Spirit to come fill you up in that area with love, peace, and joy overflowing abundantly. After you feel you have let go of that situation, ask Father God to reveal how He feels about you. You may not be hearing Father God if what you hear is not uplifting, edifying, or encouraging. I believe God has ways of correcting us that turn us away from sin and put our eyes back on Him because of the amount of love He has for each one of us. God devises ways to bring back the estranged (2 Samuel 14:14).

He is the Father of the prodigal and and is always looking for us to come running back to His arms, not from fear but because of love! Love leads people in areas fear never could. I believe that the reverential fear of God is to have such an awe of His love that we want to be obedient, like a child hanging on to Daddy's leg, wanting to go where He goes because you can't stand to not be in His presence. Grab ahold of Daddy God and don't let GO!

Prayer Declaring Victory over Fear

God, I ask that you touch the person reading (or listening to this book). I ask that you touch their heart and allow them to seek you out greater and greater every day. I pray that they will allow you to search their heart for any open doors of fear and to be open for you to remove any pain that gives the enemy a foothold in them. I ask that you would take them deeper into their heart, and that you would pour out your love over each one abundantly to heal the area after the wound is removed. God, I ask for them to receive a double portion of your love for every area where the enemy has come to steal, kill, or destroy in their lives and and even in the lives of their loved ones. God, I ask that you would show such redemption in their lives that the enemy would have no open door of fear in their life from this day forward. I ask God, that you would empower them through the Holy Spirit to keep their eyes on Jesus and to know that the power and authority that lives inside of them through you is greater than anything the enemy can send at them.

May they know that everywhere they put their feet, they claim as Kingdom territory for you, Lord God! Victory in this area of their life is Your victory, Papa God. I thank you, Father God, for protecting them in the name of Jesus! Amen.

Can our Destiny be Delayed or Changed?

Can our destiny be delayed or changed by someone else not walking in complete obedience to God? What if we don't walk in complete obedience to God, can we change or delay someone else's destiny or path in life?

I feel that God will help you answer those questions along with helping you to dig deeper into His heart to seek out vision, purpose and passion in your life.

I believe we lack three things which prevent us from being able to know what God is doing in our lives and how He wants to use us. We don't always know how to hear from God, or we hear only in pieces according to our walk with God.

Sometimes when we walk with God but choose to listen to those around us without taking it all back to God, our steps are changed and inadvertently change our own path as well as affecting the lives of those around us. Every action has a reaction! What are your actions in life and will they cause a positive or negative reaction (ripple effect) in the lives of those around you?

God will use all to His good when we allow Him Lordship of our lives and that is why it is crucial for us to build an intimate relationship with God the Father, Jesus the Son, and the Holy Spirit. Each part of the Trinity plays a different role in our lives and when we allow them to move in and through our lives, we start to build an intimate relationship that will allow us to see more clearly where the Father is so we can do what the Father is doing. Some of us allow God to move in parts of our lives, but do not seem willing to be completely open to allowing God to use every aspect of their lives. So when we only allow God to use us partly, we are more likely to filter what is being said through the other things going on in our lives.

For example, imagine you just had a very bad argument with a close friend and it is still on your mind, pulling you into a place of anger because you felt you were wronged in the situation. You can't seem to get rid of re-living situation that occurred and you don't feel you want to talk to that friend. You continue to carry that anger. At the same time, you walk in words of knowledge and God gives you prophetic words of encouragement for people and you have this urgent need inside of you to share a word with a total stranger. The urge is strong and you know it is a word from God. You deliver the word, but instead of delivering the word through the love of the Father, it is tainted by the anger and pain in your heart and the person receives a word of God delivered through your junk. Yes, God can use you despite your poor heart position because the gifts are given without repentance and are irrevocable.

We need to allow people in our lives to sow seeds into us as well as to help us stay accountable for our own actions. When we carry pain and wounds, we most likely don't see how it can affect others. If we have no vision, we are unable to see where we are going and in that, we have nothing to pray into or believe in for our future. If we see it, God says we can have it when we are in alignment with His will. I believe that vision is a key factor in our lives and that vision helps us to focus for tomorrow.

The Webster Dictionary definition of Vision is: something seen in a dream, trance, or ecstasy; *especially*: a supernatural appearance that conveys a revelation; the act or power of imagination; direct mystical awareness of the supernatural usually in visible form.

Do we know that we can use our imagination? Do we know God created us out of His own imagination and has given us the mind of Christ to use? 1 Corinthians 2:16 asks us "Who can know the LORD's thoughts? Who knows enough to teach him?" However, we can understand these things since we have the mind of Christ." Society and our culture have tried to shut down our creativity and imagination and have made us believe that it is not important and some even try to say that it is "not of God" to use our imagination. Religion has focused more on doing and working for God rather than working with God. God wants to interact with us and to "do life with us" causing our lives to be shaped. Many of the people God used in the Bible speak of the vision that God poured out to them. Without purpose, the vision is just a vision and it doesn't seem to bring to us a heart-connect with Father God.

As we understand our purpose within the vision, we can run after it with the heart of God, and believing in the vision helps us to be completely sold out for God because we see the chance to play a vital role in that piece of the future that lies before us. Webster's Dictionary defines purpose as: the reason for which something is done or created or for which something exists. We need a reason (purpose) for the vision in order to understand why we were given the vision. Sometimes we may not know the entire reason but God will give some insight to the vision to help us continue to pray into the existence of the vision for God to continue to unfold the fullness of His purpose and plans as we step into the vision.

When you understand your purpose in the vision then you can find the passion of God, the love of the Father, and run with such an understanding of it that you know that with God this vision is not too big and that it does not matter whom you were in the past. The Webster's Dictionary definition of Passion is: a term applied to a very strong feeling about a person or thing. Passion is an intense emotion, compelling enthusiasm, or desire for anything. The passion of knowing that God wants to use you to walk out a purpose in your life and that there is a vision that lays ahead of you to walk out, can help you to experience a welling up of desire inside of you to pursue it with all your heart, knowing that together with God you can walk out the vision that is in front of you, no matter how large it may seem or how insignificant you may feel.

We all (to some degree) understand that the Bible is full of people who were insignificant to the world in their day and yet God called them into mighty roles that changed nations and brought hearts back to God. The Bible is an incredible chronicle of how many people felt unworthy for the call that was on their lives and yet God chose them anyway.

Even though they hesitated as He called them and as they walked it out, God still believed in them and still pursued after them as He lifted them up above others to stand alone on His promises many times.

Vision helps you to know where He wants to take you; the places He wants to show you where He is working in your life and in the lives of those around you. Vision also helps you understand the purpose God has created you for and can cause you to look even move into the eyes of Jesus to find the passion to drive you even deeper into the arms of the Father. Vision can inspire you to be the empty vessel filled with His love, to go and be about our Father's business, completing the journey He has laid before you.

He works great miracles out of our testimonies as He sees us reach out to Him to pull us out of the mirey clay of despair and destruction because of our own choices that led us right into the plans of the enemy. He is not far, far away in Heaven, but, actually living inside of us, walking life out with us and wanting to be a part of every step in our life. We don't always realize it, but we actually choose when we allow Him to walk with us, ordering our steps. Not all of our choices are from God, even some of the ones we think are from

God. We still only hear in part, and, only see in part. What we allow into our ear and eye gates affects how we walk out our lives. As we learn how to hear more and more clearly from God, we learn to discern between several areas. When we hear from God it can at times be sifted through the emotions and thoughts of our day. You may have a great word from God, but if you have just exchanged words with another person and you are still carrying the pain and hurt of that conversation, it can cause your words to be spoken in a tone of voice that is not from God. Sometimes, even though the Word was from God, the way it was delivered was not God's heart. Wounded people wound other people all the time and it is important to not carry the emotions of others or to allow the world to influence your heart and mind.

As children of God, we have been given access to the mind of Christ with the helmet of Salvation to protect our minds and have been given the Heart of God protected by the chest plate of Righteousness. These are important pieces of your spiritual armor that should always be on you and always be protecting you from the plans of the enemy. When we make choices in our lives, God makes them work out for His greater good when we choose to trust Him to turn around what the enemy means for harm so it can be used to undo the plans of the enemy. Choose to partner with Him today!

Can Fear in Your Life Change Your Destiny?

I want to take a closer look at the scriptures to see how fear may have changed the course of the lives of Elijah and Elisha and also affected the lives of others. My heart is not to question the faith of the amazing people in the Bible. They were human just like us and sometimes allowed the enemy to hold them down in areas of their lives. Some never walked free from what held them down. I believe God shows us these things so we won't make the same mistakes or choices that bound them. I believe God shows us so we can learn from the mistakes of others and remember that if God used them, God wants to use us also. God is a God of second and third chances, and I believe He is standing right beside us, encouraging us to do well. He wants us to grow in faith, believing that this time we will overcome the enemy.

Can you picture when you learned how to ride a bike? You had this bike that looked bigger than life; With or without training wheels it looked scary. My dad was always busy working and I was blessed with my brother, Gary, who is about 10 years older than me. He put me on my bike which didn't have training wheels. My first shot at this was straight out the gate and down the hill through our yard, at the speed of sound. I don't believe I succeeded the first time, but each time I got better until I could finally ride by myself.

I feel it is like Father God is by my side helping me to ride my first bike each time I step into new areas. I put any fear under my feet and overcome that which once held me down and I can be victorious and put the enemy under my feet. God doesn't get mad at us for failing; We do that enough on our own. God is always rooting for us with His promises for us to do better the next time. He is pleased that we at least stepped out and tried to conquer the enemy. He is pleased that we are turning to Him and refusing to be held down by the strongholds that once gripped our lives.

Use your imagination to allow you to go deeper into the scriptures and stories of the Bible. They are meant to be enjoyed and are there for us to understand what the people endured and the joy they felt as their story lines unfolded. Stop reading the Bible to just read it. Camp out in the scriptures and find the heart of the Father in the midst of the stories. The Bible is full of life and it was created to help us walk out life. It was not created to be a set of Christian laws, but for us to understand the times and seasons of the stories and testimonies that pave the way for us to walk out our own lives as Christians.

We can build our faith by knowing the living God that lives inside of us. If God was with them and got them through their trials, He will most certainly be with us leading us to claim our victory.

Elijah was human just like you and I. He had fears that gripped him and sent him into hiding from Jezebel. Imagine yourself in the life of Elijah. He had just set up the enemy to fall and be destroyed as he met with King Ahab. Elijah had him summon to Mount Carmel the people from all over the land of Israel, including the 450 prophets of Baal who ate at the table of Jezebel. The duel would prove who was the true Lord God. This was bold and Elijah showed no sign of fear. It doesn't say God told Elijah he would succeed. He was walking in a faith beyond measure. Elijah had extreme confidence in challenging the prophets of Baal and his faith was rewarded by watching God Almighty, the one true living God show up and reveal Himself. The God who answered through fire on the altar would be the God of the people. These were the same people who wouldn't choose between Baal or God and stop sitting on the fence. It seems that there were many of the people torn between choosing who their God was. How many people today walk in that same place? The Baal in our life looks different. It is the idols of our lives, anything we place above God whether it be things, places, or even people in our lives; Whatever we place more importance upon than the love we have for our Lord, Jesus.

In 1 Kings 18:21, Elijah went before the people and asked, "How long will you waver between two opinions? If the LORD is God, follow him; but if Baal is God, follow him." But the people said nothing. The Hebrew for the word opinions actually means, "do you hesitate between the worship of Jehovah and of Baal?" Whom or what do we worship? What do we devote more time and energy on than God? I often pray and ask God to search my heart to reveal anything or anyone I worship greater than my Father God.

Once Elijah asked the people this, the battle was on! Baal vs Jehovah! The Prophets of Baal called upon Baal and there was no sign of him. He was a no show! They even slashed and cut themselves with swords and spears as was their custom, and still no reply from Baal. Then it was time for Elijah to prepare the altar for his sacrifice to Jehovah God. He placed twelve stones on it to precisely represent the 12 tribes from Jacob, who God called Israel. He went all out and dug a trench and filled it to overflowing with water.

The wood was drenched with water. Normally wood this wet would not light, but God Almighty can do far greater than we could ever imagine. Just picture that altar and then watch God bring on the fire to devour the sacrifice.

1 Kings 18:36-39

At the time of sacrifice, the prophet Elijah stepped forward and prayed: "LORD, the God of Abraham, Isaac and Israel, let it be known today that you are God in Israel and that I am your servant and have done all these things at your command.

Answer me, LORD; answer me, so these people will know that you, LORD, are God, and that you are turning their hearts back again."

Then the fire of the LORD fell and burned up the sacrifice, the wood, the stones and the soil, and also licked up the water in the trench.

When all the people saw this, they fell prostrate and cried, "The LORD—he is God! The LORD—he is God!"

Elijah called on the name of the LORD Almighty, the God of Abraham, Isaac, and Israel, asking God to answer him so the people would know that Jehovah is LORD God. He prayed believing that the hearts of the people would turn back to God. I would love to have seen this in person! Can you imagine the people watching? All of Israel was commanded by King Ahab to come and to see what happened and then God devoured and burned up the entire sacrifice! It even burned up the stones and soil - that was some awesome fire! The fire even licked up every drop of water! Can you just imagine that happening?!

God showed His power and turned the hearts of His people, proving who He was to those who were sitting on the fence being indecisive as to whom to worship! Jehovah showed Himself and at that moment they ALL fell prostrate crying out: "The LORD - he is God! The LORD - he is God!" Wow, more people than we could even imagine were in that one place to see the power of our Father in heaven, our Lord Jehovah, and it turned their hearts back to Him.

What an extraordinary experience Elijah encountered! He displayed such an incredible courage and confidence in God with no sign of fear, not even in front of 450 prophets of Baal. He saw God show up mightily and he should have had faith to catapult him through the rest of his days on earth. However, the next moments of his life showed a serious lack of faith in God. He allowed his fear of the words and threats of Jezebel to overpower the experience he had just encountered with the power and authority of God. Fear had an open door and it gripped him so severely that it sent him running into hiding. I believe he was then so gripped with the fear of Jezebel and his discouragement from failing God that he couldn't pull himself out of the depths of depression! He didn't have any person beside him to help him see where he was struggling even though God was with him. However, God will not go against our free will. Elijah had to take charge of his life and he alone was responsible for his actions. We chose the path in our own lives.

God will not force us to do what He has planned for our destiny. Every action in our lives has a reaction and there is always a consequence stemming from what we choose. Good or bad!

How many times do we see God move mightily in our lives and then still doubt when something hard comes along? In a moment we seem lose our faith that God is greater than any circumstance in our life. I saw God move mightily in my life while spending over 2 months in Brazil. God opened up opportunity after opportunity to minister and I saw His power and authority move; I saw blind eyes open, a deaf ear open, and a major deliverance where the enemy used a man's voice in English tell me I didn't know what I was doing but I saw God deliver and set free that young girl in an instant. Despite seeing all these awesome miracles with my own eyes while in Brazil, when I returned to the United States, I was shut down like a little school girl.

It took me about 9 months to get rid of the offense I took on through that experience. The enemy does attack and he can and will use close friends at times to offend us after having an incredible experience where we see God move mightily. We are not any different than Elijah, and God still took care of him. God still loved him unconditionally despite him responding in fear to the threats of Jezebel. God did not throw him into the hands of Jezebel. He still protected and provided for Elijah's every need. God even sent him to Horeb, the mountain of God. Even in the midst of his melt down, God still was gentle and kind to him! God didn't give up on Elijah even when Elijah gave up on himself. God even entrusted Elijah with the lives of three men even after Elijah's moment of defeat and hiding in a cave. God believed in him, just as He believes in you and me. God will not stop using you even when you have fallen and are in a place where you think you want to die. God would far rather have us let Him help us with our wounds and close the doors to where the enemy wants to attack us.

I believe the trials and tribulations we go through are like scripture spoken of in James 1 where it says that we should consider it pure joy whenever we face trials of many kinds, because the testing of our faith produces perseverance. James says to allow the perseverance to finish its work so that you may be "mature and complete, not lacking anything". We are to ask for wisdom when we lack wisdom and God will give generously to all without finding fault. James also says when you ask, you must believe and not doubt (one who doubts is like a wave of the sea, blown and tossed by the wind), and that the double-minded person who doubts should not expect anything from the Lord. Persevering under a trial is blessed because when you have stood the test, you will receive a crown of life that the Lord has promised to those who love Him. James explains that most people blame God for the temptations in their lives. Temptations are not from God for God cannot be tempted by evil, or does he tempt anyone. When we are tempted it is because of our own evil desires that entice us. As we consider that temptation and receive it into our hearts, it conceives and gives birth to sin and when that sin is full grown, it gives birth to death. James also says that every good and perfect gift is from above, coming down from the Father of lights who does not change like shifting shadows.

This scripture helps us to understanding that the negative inside of us is not from God and that God wants to remove it for us. He wants to free us from all the pain and wounds of yesterday if we would just be willing to let go of our past and let God show us our future.

Even though Elijah ran and hid from Jezebel, God still wanted to restore him and use him. God tasked him with anointing 3 men. I believe there was a specific order that he was to carry out his assignment since the scripture speaks of it twice in 1 Kings 19:15- 17.

The LORD said to him, "Go back the way you came, and go to the Desert of Damascus. When you get there, anoint Hazael king over Aram.

Also, anoint Jehu son of Nimshi king over Israel, and anoint Elisha son of Shaphat from Abel Meholah to succeed you as prophet.

Jehu will put to death any who escape the sword of Hazael, and Elisha will put to death any who escape the sword of Jehu.

God specifies to Elijah to go back the way he came to the Desert of Damascus and he specifies to anoint Hazael king over Aram, then anoint Jehu king over Israel, and then anoint Elisha to succeed Elijah as prophet. I believe it was this order because in the last scripture above it says that Jehu will put to death any who escape the sword of Hazael and Elisha will put to death any who escape the sword of Jehu. However, did Elijah go back by the way that he came through the desert of Damascus? I don't believe he did that when it says he went right to find Elisha. Elisha was to succeed Elijah as prophet and I believe he saw an end to his struggles. This is what causes me to feel that we can shift or change destiny in our own lives and the lives of others when we are not completely obedient to the Lord. I believe when Elijah told Elisha: "Go Back, what have I done to you?" It might have been that God opened his eyes to see what he had just done. What if he felt the anointing lift off of him and transfer onto Elisha? What if he realized that he wouldn't fulfill the destiny on earth that God had for him? I would like to propose that because it took another 11-12 years at least before Elisha anointed Hazael and had an unknown prophet anoint Jehu that many lives were changed in those years. Many destinies were shifted. What if many people even died without knowing the one, true God? I am not putting Elijah down, rather I am just proposing that if God still used him mightily after this event, we should keep in mind that God can still use us when we screw up.

Elisha actually burned his plow to roast the oxen he had been plowing with when Elijah anointed him. He was sold out to God and kissed his family good-bye to follow after Elijah. He was instantly changed when Elijah threw his cloak around him. When that mantel from God hit Elisha, I believe there was no way he could continue to just plow fields. His life was forever changed in that moment and I believe he actually felt Jehovah place the mantel on him and give him the power and authority to walk out the call on his life. What if that was you? Would you be willing to kill all your oxen and burn your plow and kiss you family good-bye? Could you say "Yes" if God would do that to you? What would that look like today? Imagine you are a young businessman with the world in your hands and very successful working on Wall Street making millions of dollars and somebody doesn't even ask, but places a mantel from God on you! Could you say good-bye to your family and your job? Elisha walked away from everything - he didn't sell it and take the money with him. Could you walk away from everything to the degree that you would not have a job to come back to if things didn't work out? Could you walk away from everything not knowing where you were going or, more importantly, if you would even like what you would be doing? What about all your electronics, your phone, your finances, your house, and maybe even your own family?

Peter and the disciples all did the same thing Elisha did; Jesus stood on the shore and said to them, "come follow me". Who was this person? Why would I leave something good to go where I don't know where I would even be going or even how I could live financially? In January 2012 I encountered this same question from God! I was at a conference and was slain in the Spirit during impartation. While on the floor during an encounter with God, He told me to get rid of EVERYTHING! Everything is what He said, nothing more and nothing less! Wow! Did I really hear you God? So I got up off the floor and went to talk to friends of mine at the conference, to tell them what I just encountered. Before I even spoke my friend Sherri said these words that forever changed my life. She said, "I don't know what you just encountered, but there is a banner over your heard that is white with black letters spelling CRUCIAL"! I collapsed in her arms with tears streaming down my face, thinking to myself "God you are serious". Then she told me these words that took me over two years to walk out: "you do not feel worthy for the call that is on your life". I was undone and a sobbing mess! God spoke and then gave me confirmation within minutes without my friend knowing anything about what He had just told me.

That year I was planning a trip in March of 2012 Brazil with Global Awakening. Before I left, God told me to tell my landlord (my brother) that I would be moving out by the end of June. I did not know where I would go, but God said to tell him before I left for Brazil. I broke down as I told him two days before leaving for Brazil. My one close friend who was also my mentor felt it was crazy to tell him right before going away for so long. She said I didn't have to give my brother that much notice, however, I felt I needed to because I had to walk out obedience to God. This experience with my mentor was really iron sharpening iron!

When I first came back from Brazil, I was speaking at a church one morning and God told me while looking in a mirror these words which I will never forget! God said, "I am serious about you getting rid of everything." Oh my gawrsh, He really is really serious! The crazy thing with all of this is that my Mom had just passed away in October of 2011 and she had left everything to me in her Will. I was the only one living with my Mom at the time and only really had my own car. Now I had all kinds of household goods that completely filled a one car garage and lived in a beautiful two bedroom townhouse. I had my own place at last and a good job that paid my bills with money so that I could sow into other ministries. I was loving being on my own. Suddenly walking away from everything seemed crazy and didn't make any sense to the world. I could almost feel the questions people were thinking and I definitely heard their concerns about my doing this.

God told me to give a 5 week notice at my job at the end of May. Oh my gawrsh, people really thought I was losing it. I was walking away from my job and my home. Not only was I walking away from what I had known for so many years, I didn't have any clue where I was going or what I would be doing. To most people this was scary and definitely was not wisdom. I heard many comment: "God wouldn't take you out of one job without having something else lined up." God can and God was taking me out of my safe environment and I had to step without seeing anything for the future. Crazy! I was sold out to be in complete alignment with God and I was not looking back.

Although God lined up a place for me to stay a week before I was moving out, I feel I actually missed the greatest opportunity. A close friend of mine was just graduating from high school and heading to a three week intensive school at Global Awakening and then three days after the school ended she was heading to Tanzania, Africa. I really felt I had a word from God to go for the 3 weeks to Africa, but that opportunity was missed because I allowed fear to come into my heart. Hearing all of the fear from others started to work on my heart and looking at my checking account and seeing the money going down, stirred more fear in me. How could I do this? How could I go half way around the world to another country when I didn't have any money? When push comes to shove, you learn what is inside of you. You also learn what you take on that is not yours.

As I walked out the next 6 months of my life, there were not a lot of opportunities for me to speak and I was questioning what God was doing. First I moved about 3 hours away and then God opened a door to move closer to where I had lived, but I stilled lived in an area that was not cost effective towards getting a job. Every time I would ask God about working, He showed me His provision in crazy ways. However, there were many nights when I cried myself to sleep. One night when I felt the pressures of all the questions about what I was doing, I heard the words of the scripture which says you should have an honest job to earn an honest living. People spoke words, not intending to hurt me, but the words were still hurtful, and I would feel they thought I was waiting on a handout or that I felt I was owed something. If they only truly knew my heart and knew what God was saying to me, they would understand God was building my faith to trust Him for my provision in every way.

I was living about 3 hours away from where I grew up when I really began to struggle financially. I felt the pressures of others who were concerned about where I would end up when my money ran out. I cried myself to sleep one night praying and asking God if I really was to get a job. I told him I was not above working and would get a job, but that I just needed direction since God had me living in an area that was not close to any stores or business. The very next morning "Grandpa", an elderly man whom I was helping, slid two $50 bills across the counter at breakfast. He didn't know my prayers or my concerns. He said "These are not from me. I would love to give them to you, but they are from your Papa God and he wants to show you He will provide for you." What do you do except know it was God? As I reached for the money, tears were streaming down my face. God was hearing me and I was walking this out in faith and I was right in the middle of His will. Over the last several years God has showed me His provision time after time in so many ways. My heart is for you to walk where God is calling you and not simply give in to what the world expects of you. Sometimes it looks impossible to do what God is calling you to do. However, I know if God calls you out, His word says He will guide your steps. It might not be easy, but God never said it would be easy. He just said to come follow me!

Fear still gripped Elisha and he finally sent an unknown prophet to anoint Jehu rather than going to anoint Jehu himself. He even told him to "not delay" and "to flee quickly." I believe it was fear that spoke out that warning. Sometimes God will send someone else to do what you are called to do if you allow fear to cause you to not to speak the words God gives you for them.

> 2 Kings 9:3
>
> "Then take the flask of oil, and pour *it* on his head, and say, 'Thus says the LORD: "I have anointed you king over Israel." ' Then open the door and flee, and do not delay."

Since Elisha sent an unknown prophet to anoint Jehu, he struggled to believe the words that the unknown prophet had spoken to him and it took his fellow officers to announce that Jehu was King. I feel that sometimes we can miss fulfilling an assignment on time and God will send someone else in our place.

> 2 Kings 9:6-8
>
> Then he arose and went into the house. And he poured the oil on his head, and said

to him, "Thus says the LORD God of Israel: 'I have anointed you king over the people of the LORD, over Israel.

'You shall strike down the house of Ahab your master, that I may avenge the blood of My servants the prophets, and the blood of all the servants of the LORD, at the hand of Jezebel.

'For the whole house of Ahab shall perish; and I will cut off from Ahab all the males in Israel, both bond and free.

If the unknown prophet had done exactly what Elisha said to do, would Jezebel have been overthrown? Sometimes we have to make a choice in life over whether to adhere to man or to God, and sometimes that is going to go against our leader's wishes. I believe that the more time you spend with God and listen to what He has to say, the greater your ability will be to discern when you are hearing from God and or hearing your own voice or that of another. Pray continually, asking God to search your heart and to show you any areas that are not of Him, that is the greatest way to keep your heart pure. One prayer that is powerful is to ask Him to reveal any pride, jealousy, anger, resentment, control, fear, or unforgiveness in your heart, and then ask Him to remove the root cause of the open door so that all the doors to the enemy in your life can be closed fully.

God is all about Relationships
David and Absalom

I have been blessed with amazing friends ever since I started to really walk with God. My first Mentor (and Best Friend) helped me understand many things God has been doing in my life. There is one thing that stands out: She taught me early into my walk to not be looking at her, but rather to look to God. In that, she has showed me that each time I step away from a person or place, I need to have my eyes on God. This has helped me as I talk with others. I want them to have their eyes on God as well, and not just following anything I say. We all need to always bring things back to God to learn what He wants us to know in each instance.

God showed me scripture where David took his eyes off of God and listened to his men instead of consulting God and it cost him his son Absalom's life. David was depressed because Absalom had killed his brother, Ammon, for sleeping with their sister, Tamar. At that time in his life, David didn't have Jonathan or Samuel to help counsel him. I feel it is important to always have people alongside of us to help us stay in alignment with God. Sometimes when we get out of alignment, we are unable to see it ourselves. Sometimes it takes someone else to speak into our life to keep us in check. We need to continue to allow people to speak into our lives and to stay in a place where we are teachable and able to receive what others say while continually taking it all back to God. Imagine being David - unable to deal with the death of your son, Ammon, who was killed by your other son, Absalom. Ammon raped Tamar and causing an anger to brew inside of Absalom because of the devastation his sister, both physically and emotionally. Absalom let the anger stew for over two years while he waited for his father, David, to rectify the situation until Absalom could stand it no longer and he had Ammon killed by his servants.

Several years later, David finally let Absalom come home, but would not look at him and didn't interact with him. It was as if he was dead to David.

Rebellion rose up inside of Absalom to the point that he wanted his father David's kingdom and they went to battle over it and David was ready to fight against his son. This part is the interesting part of the story: David's men spoke to him, saying that it would be better for him to stay back and not go to battle with his men, against Absalom.

2 Samuel 18:3-4

But the men said, "You must not go out; if we are forced to flee, they won't care about us. Even if half of us die, they won't care; but you are worth ten thousand of us. It would be better now for you to give us support from the city."

King David answered, "I will do whatever seems best to you." So the King stood beside the gate while all his men marched out in units of hundreds and thousands.

Instead of David taking the word of his men back to God, he said to his men "I will do whatever seems best to you." How many times do we take a word from someone and not go back to God to see if it truly is from Him? I hear people prophesying to people as if giving a Word and saying it was God, when all along they actually knew something of the situation; I call that the Spirit of Obvious. I see people hang on those Words, believing the Word exactly as it was spoken over them. I don't like to prophesy over someone I know or in an area that I already know about in their life. I rarely accept a Word from someone who knows me, especially if that Word is in regards to something they are already aware of in my life. I want confirmations to come from people who have no clue as to what is going on in my life or at least the area of my life, which they are prophesying over.

As Absalom headed into battle against David's men, his mule took him under the thick boughs of a great oak and Absalom's head was caught fast in a fork of the oak's branches. The mule under him ran away, leaving Absalom hanging between the heavens and the earth. Let's think about this for a moment. Visualize being caught in the fork of a great oak. In Isaiah 61 it speaks of the oaks of righteousness which are planted by God Himself. What if Absalom was in the hand of God, hanging between heaven and earth awaiting his fate. What if David had gone to God to ask Him if he should even go to battle against Absalom? What if David would have gone to God about actually going to battle with his men and he had been on the battlefield that day?

I would like to propose that God was waiting on David to come and rescue his son.

The revelation God showed me in these scriptures is that the hand of God was holding Absalom and waiting for David to rescue him. However, David was listening to others and had not consulted with God, so David missed one of the greatest opportunities ever to see his prodigal son come home.

What does this look like today in our own society?

Picture a young man raised in a really great home. This young man has loving parents and incredible potential in life. One day he and his brother are out on a joy ride with two friends and have a little too much to drink. All of a sudden, the car loses control and a horrific accident unravels before their eyes. Absalom is the son who is the driver and lives through the accident while Ammon and two other friends die in the accident.

Hearts are broken and lives are shattered by the horrific accident. Absalom is injured badly and has life threatening injuries. His parents are heart broken and in despair and don't know how deal with this tragedy. They are grieving over both sons, one critically injured and the other dead, and the enemy pulls them into the deep darkness of oppression and depression. They are gripped with anger and unforgiveness towards Absalom because he was the oldest and was highly intoxicated. He was living his life recklessly and now he has involved his little brother to the point where it killed him. What do you do as parents? How do you get out of the darkness of the pit you feel like you have fallen into?

David is the father and also has choices to make, yet he is so grieved with the pain of losing his youngest son that he can't see past the pain and forgive the oldest son who is laying in the hospital hanging on for his own life. He can't bring himself to go to the hospital and his friends are angry as well because they also lost their sons and are grieving. He is not hearing any encouragement to reach out to his son, Absalom, so he allows the grief to hold him in bondage. This pain keeps him from walking into the hospital room where his oldest son, the one he has never connected with, the one that has always been rebellious and troubled, but was really always, looking for his father's acceptance.

The son is in a coma and in the hands of the Almighty Father, waiting on David to come speak life into him, but David doesn't come. No matter how much love the mother gives, the son still longs for the father to appreciate him and to love him for who he is and to no longer judge him because he is different.

Absalom is fading fast because he has lost all hope of believing his father truly loves him. He hears what people are speaking even though he is in a coma. He hears the words which are spoken about Ammon dying in the car accident and that he was responsible. How can he ever fix that problem, when he has screwed up everything he has ever laid his hands on throughout his life? The young man, Absalom, dies without hearing his father say "I love you!" His life hung on those words and his wounded heart and lack of hope opened the door to the enemy to destroy him completely; His body was unable to heal because there was no hope in his life.

David, the father, never meant for Absalom to be distant from him. He loved him the only way he knew how to love; He loved his son the same way he was loved by his father. His father was hard on him also and believed in David far more than David believed in himself, but his father never said he loved him nor did he show David any love. His son was so much like him that they didn't know how to communicate. The difference was that David in his younger years learned how to persevere through life as he was out on his own, building his career. He found great success and wanted his son to have the character to take over someday as his oldest son; David was hard on young Absalom so that he would be strong and bold enough to take over the business someday.

How many times can you picture a similar scenario? Have you ever wanted love or acceptance from a Mother or Father or someone else in your life yet never received it? Sometimes we never understand why people can't show us love even though they really do love us. What will you do in your life differently so that the "Absaloms" in your life are not left hanging?

God loves us so much and He forgives us each time we go to Him in true repentance with a pure heart. He believes in us and encourages us to succeed and walk out our destiny with Him, not just for Him. He says to forgive 70 times 7 and He also says 7 times in one day. He wants us to love our enemies and the two commandments He gave us were to "Love God with all our heart, mind, soul, and strength" and to "love our neighbors as we love ourselves."

We struggle with both because it takes loving ourselves to be able to love. We love to the degree that we have been taught to love. When you see an angry person, take a moment to pray for them and know that maybe they are loving to the degree they love themselves, and that is not at all.

I believe the church as a whole has felt that the ones who see life and God differently are rebellious because we don't just go along with the way things have always been done. We are a generation who just can't understand why people just go along with something because it is the way it has always been done. Some people know if they stand up to the old traditions and go with their heart that rejection could result and that scares them to death. They remain miserable in their own lives instead of standing up for something that touches their hearts. I believe this has created plastic people in the church who wear a facade while in Church and around their Church friends.

In reality, their lives and families are dying on the inside and are on the very brink of destruction. They slowly spiritually die and lose all hope!

I experienced the Hand of God in an encounter a few years ago. I have struggled on occasion walking out my walk, questioning not working and wondering what full-time ministry looks like. I have people continue to ask me if I should just get a job. It does wear on you, especially when it comes from people you highly respect and those who walk in authority, and close friends or family whom you love. I really started to doubt what I was doing because I was down to my last $20. I was driving home from Ohio, not sure if I really had enough gas and toll money, but believing God was providing. I started to entertain the idea of looking for a job even though I know each time I have do me that, God has shown me something else and reminded me that "where He is taking me, He is building great faith in me" because He says that "where I am going, I will need to trust Him and to have great faith." That hurts, building great faith, because it is a stretching of everything I know. He has also said He would teach me through experiences because we tend to forget the amazing things God does at times when you are being stretched the greatest.

I was in a Church service and went down under the power of God during prayer time and God took me into an encounter. During the encounter, my body was laying in a grave and my spirit was up above the grave trying to get to my body. I was so frustrated and at my wits end because the devil was standing in front of me and wouldn't let me get to my body in the grave. I was standing there and tears were streaming down my face as I watched the devil throw dirt in on my body, I even felt myself suffocating. Not a pleasant feeling. I really felt like I couldn't breathe! I crouched down and put my arms around my knees and my head in my hands and gave it all up to God and said, "God, I need your help!" As soon as I said "Help", Jesus walked out of the grave with my body in His arms. I knew in my spirit I was going to be okay. Jesus looked at me and said, "it is not your own". I felt this amazing refreshed and restored feeling flood my body with an incredibly intense peace washing over me. It was so amazing and I was not concerned anymore. As I lay there, a sobbing mess, God spoke to me and I won't forget what He said to me. God said: "Stop adhering to what man says!" If I don't stop adhering to what man says, this is what will truly happen to me: I will lose all hope; I will lose my passion; I will then lose my purpose; and finally I will lose my vision. He said that "without passion, purpose, and vision" I will spiritually die and that will open the door to the enemy attacking me everywhere I have been healed; Everything I was healed of would come back with a vengeance.

You may be asking "Where that is in scripture?" Or maybe even thinking "That wouldn't happen!" Oh, but I believe God was real that day and I heard Him loud and clear. The scripture that comes to me is when Jesus heals the man at the pool of Bethesda and the next day He sees him in the Temple and says to him: "you have been healed; stop sinning or something worse may happen to you." (John 5:14)

In my case, I would be walking in direct disobedience to God because I know He had me leave my job and has me walking out a faith journey where building a ministry with Him. Working, in my case, would be sin because it would be in disobedience to God.

People struggle for many reasons, but you cannot take on their worry, their doubt, or even their jealousy. You have to know without a doubt what God is saying in your life and that it is from Him and not just a "feel good" Word from someone else. Use what others say as confirmation of what God is saying to you. God is about relationship and He wants us to commune with Him all the time, not just when we are in trouble.

Claiming Our Inheritance and Stepping into our Promised Land

God pouring out revelation through His Word is vital to our knowing who He is to us. I get so excited to just open up the scriptures and ask Papa: "Where do you want to take me today?" I have no agenda nor do I focus on reading in any certain place or reading any set amount. I love it when you are just opening up the Bible with no rhyme or reason and you just start to read and God shows you answers to your questions or to prayers you have been praying. You see the scriptures come to life and speak to your heart. This happens to me the majority of my time reading the scriptures. I see the Holy Spirit bring it to life and that is how I have been "remembering" the stories; they mean something in my heart and they become one with my heart. The enemy can't take it away from you then because there is now a "heart connect" and it was not there is now just something you read because someone or some religion told you that you had to read a certain amount of your Bible on a given day.

My prayer for you is that God will use this book to help the scriptures open up to you in a whole new way. I pray that He opens your eyes and ears more to see the Bible come alive like you have never encountered it before. There is so much God has hidden in the scriptures and that amazes me each time I read it. You can go to the same scripture and He can talk to you about it in a brand new way! We are in exciting times and on the precipice of seeing Him reveal His hidden mysteries more and more to those who will search them out.

God showed me an incredible analogy within the Baptism of Jesus a few years ago. He gave me this revelation over a period of time. He would reveal more and more of the story as if it was still unraveling in my heart. I continue to chew on this revelation in amazement of how there is such purpose to what we do and where we go. He has been showing me to continue to be alert and watch for the little things and He will highlight even the smallest movement of Him to me. I just need to stay alert!

This revelation came while I was studying the Book of Joshua as I was writing my first sermon while I attended the Global School of Supernatural Ministry (GSSM). This was before we were sent out into the Nation (USA) on practicum (10-12 weeks of teaching and preaching all over the US and into Canada). I was stepping into new territory and I was excited to jump in with both feet.

I had only been really walking with God for about 2 ½ years at this point. The only time I had ever spoken in front of large group was a year earlier to give my testimony. Before that, you would not have found me in front of even a small group to speak; it scared me to death to speak to any size group, and to even read in a small setting. I would fret and find ways to get out of talking. I was embarrassed by my reading which was only at about an 8th grade level even after graduating High School. My speech was not much better. Reading, English, and Speech Classes were my worst subjects and it got worse when I was separated out in school to attend a special reading class - I wasn't special. I felt dumb and that just added to my embarrassment and reinforced my low self-esteem.

While attending GSSM, God poured out His goodness so mightily! I want to give credit to Ben Williams (staff at GSSM) for his teaching which stirred my heart to dive into the scriptures. I started to meditate on scripture and chew it up until I understood what God was saying to me. I watched God unveil so much revelation as He created a hunger inside of me that has never really stopped. I pray God continues to stir up and increase the hunger inside of you to go after the mysteries hidden within the scriptures.

Have you ever wondered "why did God choose the Jordon River to have Jesus Baptized?" He could have chosen many different bodies of water, even the Sea of Galilee. I would like to propose this thought to you: Maybe the reason God chose the Jordon was because it represented the death of Christ to come.

God had me dive into the concordance where I find out the meaning behind the words:

- Jordon River- the Descender; the Jordon flows into the Dead Sea

- The Dead Sea is a sea with no life because of its high salt content

Matthew 5:13 tells us that ***"You are the salt of the earth"***.

- We are the salt of the earth!
- God called Joshua to cross over the Jordon and not go through the Jordon because God was going to put the enemy under his feet as he crossed over the Jordan into his Promised land.

Joshua 1:11 instructed them to: ***"Prepare your provisions, for within three days you shall pass over this Jordan to go in to take possession of the land which the Lord your God is giving you to possess."***
Joshua 3:15 warns them, ***"For the Jordan overflows all its banks throughout the time of harvest"***

- He and those who bore the Ark of the Covenant stepped into the flood waters and when the soles of their feet rested in the Jordon, the waters coming from above were cut off.

They were to keep their eyes on the Ark (God) and not to look to the left or the right, but keep their eyes forward which means we can't be looking to our past either (it isn't ours)! [Lot and his family were told to not look back and when his wife was disobedient and looked back, she turned into a pillar of salt that is there still to this day!]

Matthew 22:44 tells us that Father God said to Jesus, *"Sit at My right hand until I put Your enemies under your feet". As we step into the enemy camp, he is cut off and we claim territory everywhere we step says The Lord God Almighty.*

The enemy is under our feet!

- The Dead Sea is downstream of us

We are called to not look to the left or the right, but to keep our eyes on the Ark (Jesus)

- When you take your eyes off of Jesus, you get caught up in chaos of the enemy and swept downstream into the Dead Sea
- ***Isaiah 60:5** states: "then you shall see and be radiant, and your heart shall thrill and tremble with joy and be enlarged; because the abundant wealth of the [Dead Sea] shall be turned to you, unto you shall the nations come with their treasures."*

God showed me that as we cross the Jordan carrying our dreams and visions, we can get distracted by the enemy and take our eyes off Jesus. When we lose our footing, we get swept down the Jordan into the Dead Sea, and we are stuck there. Many people, along with their dreams and visions are in the Dead Sea waiting on the Sons and Daughters to help them get free; they help us refocus on Jesus and be restored back to who they were created to be. Once again we can be on our journey with our new found love and be rejuvenated because we know we are treasures that were lost but now are found!

So how about this thought to chew on: Jesus was baptized in the Jordon which means the "descender"! We know that when He went down in the Jordan during His baptism, it represented death and as He came up, it represented life everlasting! So Jesus being baptized in the Jordon represented the true death of sin on the cross to defeat death's hold on man. As He was raised up after His baptism, the Holy Spirit descended upon Him in bodily form signifying His resurrection through new spiritual life. What if we truly die to our old self during baptism, and it is not just a pretend, symbolic death! Our old life truly has passed away and we truly are a new being! Hence the term "Born Again Christian".

During our baptism the Holy Spirit descends upon us in the same way it happened with Jesus.

I believe Jesus was fully a man. He freely chose to lay aside His deity so that He could be our example as He walked on the earth. To be able to follow someone, we need to have the same opportunities and capabilities as that person. I believe Jesus laid aside his deity and chose to walk out his destiny on earth as a man rightly aligned with God's heart. I believe during his baptism God Almighty entered him through the Holy Spirit. The Holy Spirit then led Jesus into the wilderness for 40 days where He was tempted by Satan. I believe He couldn't have been tempted otherwise, because James 1 states that God cannot be tempted by evil.

If you are full of something, it is one thing or the other. It can't be both, so Jesus was either fully God or fully man. The Bible does not say He was both. As we follow Jesus, we need to fully accept Him as our Lord and Savior. We need to ask Him into our heart and not just pray a "feel good" prayer, but actually make a heart connect with Jesus as we choose to make Him the Lord of our lives. I believe we then need to ask the Spirit of God to fill us with His spirit just as Jesus breathed on the Disciples in the Upper Room and as the

Spirit fell on everyone with tongues of fire on Pentecost which empowered them with the Spirit of God bringing them His power and authority. Our Water Baptism seals the deal on our accepting Jesus - I believe it represents our total transformation with the death of our old man and the birth of our new man! By faith, the Holy Spirit also descends upon us during our baptism whether we see it or not with our natural eyes. By faith we receive. I believe these three components – receiving Jesus as Lord and Savior, water baptism, and Baptism of the Spirit - are vital to our success in walking out our destiny.

Here are some thoughts to consider:

- When we accept Jesus as our Lord and Savior, it is Jesus coming into our lives and that relationship is the start! He goes to the Father and intercedes on our behalf!
- When we are baptized by the Holy Spirit, the Spirit of God infills us and brings us the comforter, along with the power and authority of the Almighty God in Spirit form.
- When we are water baptized, God descends upon us and resides inside of each of us. Our body then truly becomes the Temple of God.

What if when Jesus prayed to the Father in John 17, His prayer was truly for us to be one with Him as He is one with the Father. What if that prayer is truly answered through the help of the Holy Spirit bringing it all together. We need to really know that it is not just us in our body, that Jesus as well as God resides inside of us! Wouldn't the world act differently and wouldn't we act differently if we knew Who really was inside of us? Knowing that should give us reverential Fear of the Lord, where we would want nothing other than to honor Him, Jesus, and the Holy Spirit, with all of our actions especially how we treat our bodies!

I have been really praying and asking God to show me more! One day, I felt God direct me to read Isaiah 5. I started there and continued on through Chapters 6 and 7. The scriptures really opened up, causing me to have a greater appreciation of Jesus by knowing that Jesus freely chose to have the same limitations as we do as people.

Isaiah 7:14-16:

Therefore the Lord Himself will give you a sign: The virgin will conceive and give birth to a son, and will call Him Immanuel. He will be eating curds and honey when He knows enough to reject the wrong and choose the right, for before the boy knows enough to reject the wrong and choose the right, the land of the two kings you dread will be laid waste.

Yes, you are reading correctly! This scripture is talking about Jesus being born to Mary! It talks about how Jesus needed to learn to "reject the wrong and choose the right". If Jesus was fully God, He would not have needed to learn to reject the wrong and chose the right. This is stated twice so we don't overlook this important scripture.

The Concordance says:

- Know: to perceive and see, find out and discern; to know by experience; Hebrew-Chaldee Lexicon says "to perceive, to acquire knowledge, to know, to be acquainted."
- Curds: Hebrew-Chaldee Lexicon says "curdled milk, such milk having an intoxicating power."

We also need to learn right from wrong! I knew kids as I was growing up that had a purity about them and I don't think they had the ability to sin. They were just different! Maybe that is the same way Jesus was. The scripture says that it was only after Jesus knew to reject the wrong and to chose the right that he would be given access to curds and honey; Jesus would receive access to the intoxicating power of God only after He knew to reject wrong and choose right. It was only after Jesus had fulfilled all the law put forth in the Old Testament, that He was found to be righteous in God's eyes. He had to fulfill all of the laws of the Old Testament so that God could accord Him righteousness and He could then become the sacrifice to atone for mankind's sin. He could only serve as the sacrifice for our sins by being a man who was completely pure and found to be without sin. Jesus was sent on a mission by God to redeem man by bringing the Kingdom of God back to earth in order to re-establish man's dominion over Satan. In order to accomplish that, Jesus had to learn right from wrong so that he could walk in the authority as a man rightly aligned with God's heart. We have trouble believing that God came to earth just to save us. There is so much more to that process and why God chose to set us free through the free will of Jesus; He won't force us to want a relationship with Him, but that is one of His greatest desires.

I have another thought which is not doctrine, but just me thinking out loud. What if it is true that God knew us before we were formed in our mother's womb? The scripture says in Jeremiah 1:5

"Before I formed you in the womb I knew you, before you were born I set you apart; I appointed you as a prophet to the nations."

He knew us before we were even born and God is all about relationship. That relationship was strong and He set you apart. What if together with God we agreed to come to earth because we knew that we could overcome everything the enemy threw our way. When I consider this, I begin to really think. I also had to learn right from wrong - it took me a little longer than Jesus and I am still a work in progress. Jesus is tangible to me. It is like when you see an older brother overcome a battle in his life and it gives you confidence to overcome the same opposition in life. The opposition is the battle, no matter what it looks like. Our battle is against the enemy and we need to use our power and the authority of God who lives inside of us to keep the enemy under our feet. I believe there is so much revelation in these Chapters in Joshua. I believe God unravels revelation to show us how to walk into our own promised land.

God tells us to arise and become powerful (Joshua 1:1-2). Arise means to choose to come into being (come into life).

- Arise è6905 **(quwm) küm:** to arise; become powerful; choose to stand in order to receive
- Arise è(dict) Come into being (come into life)
- Being è(dict) life

Isaiah 60:1 says to Shine and that we are the light of Christ and God is calling us to let the light within us to shine. God is calling us forth to wake up and change our position by standing up for what we believe. This is part of finding passion, purpose, and vision within our lives, and understanding that we have a destiny that is greater than anything we could ever dream or dare to imagine.

God was calling Joshua to arise after the death of Moses and take his place! God is still calling forth the "Joshuas" to step into leadership, to arise and change positions in their lives by taking ownership of who they are in Christ. We can't receive our promised land if we are not standing up. Being rightly aligned with God and having our eyes focused on Jesus while allowing ourselves to be guided and directed by the Holy Spirit are all essential to our lives as Christians.

God had groomed both Joshua and Caleb for years before taking their journey into the Promised Land; they themselves were ready 40 years earlier. I believe there are some of you reading this who God may be talking to directly. God is calling you forward to step in as leaders. Is it now your season to step into something you thought had died? I hope you don't think you are too old - Caleb was 80 years old and felt as young as he did when he was 20 when Moses first told him of the promised land that he would inherit. He waited years alongside Joshua while Joshua led and claimed his own territory. It was then finally time for Caleb to step into his promises and I believe it is a now season for you to step into your promises as well. However, it is important for you to take everything back to God to discover His truth for your own life - do not just rely on my word to you.

God told Joshua that He was with Moses and that He (God) would also be with Joshua. God is the same yesterday, today, and tomorrow! Joshua and Caleb carried a different Spirit from the rest of the Israelites and I believe it was the same Holy Spirit we carry today once we receive the Baptism in the Spirit. So if God was with them, He is also with us!

He will not forsake you nor will He fail you! He calls us to "be strong and of good courage" and I believe each one of you reading or listening to this book is also called forth to lead others, encouraging them to also inherit their promised land. What if as we step out of our comfort zone, we start to run after the things of God and really start to be real with others in our lives. We must purpose our hearts on God and run with passion towards the visions and dreams God pours into us, not allowing man to stop us or to cause us to doubt. We are conquerors and not grasshoppers. I know that I myself want to walk into my promises from God and claim my territory to inherit my promised land. I don't want to allow fear of others to cause me to become full of fear to the point where I stop and sit. Not even for a bit! I feel the promised land is knowing our true identity in Christ and jumping into the Spirit of God wholly and sold out, running with access to all of the tools, knowledge, and wisdom of God. With God we can free the captives, unleashing the chains of their bondages.

I hear people say there is a cost and they don't know if they want to pay the price. I say that the price was so large that He sent His only son to die for you and me. There can't be a higher price!

I also believe that if we walk where we are called, our families will also come into alignment. I heard a testimony of a lady a few years ago and she wanted her son to walk beside her in ministry, but he wasn't anywhere close. She was afraid her boldness would cause him to go backwards, stepping away from God and that he would even reject her. She finally started to step into where God was calling her and today her son is beside her in ministry just like she prayed. So I should be who God is calling me to be, no matter the cost and know who I am in Christ. I must trust and believe God for all the rest around me. I must love them where they are, honoring and respecting them for who they are and not for who I want them to become.

I want to walk out Isaiah 61 because God told Isaiah that he was anointed and qualified and so are you!

Isaiah 61:1-3

The Spirit of the Sovereign LORD is on me, because the LORD has anointed me to proclaim good news to the poor. He has sent me to bind up the brokenhearted, to proclaim freedom for the captives and release from darkness for the prisoners, to proclaim the year of the LORD's favor and the day of vengeance of our God, to comfort all who mourn, and provide for those who grieve in Zion— to bestow on them a crown of beauty instead of ashes, the oil of joy instead of mourning, and a garment of praise instead of a spirit of despair. They will be called oaks of righteousness, a planting of the LORD for the display of his splendor.

As we walk forward, even if the enemy causes you to stumble, don't hide your mistakes. Allow people to see you get your eyes back on Jesus and walk it out standing tall and overcoming that thing that caused you to stumble yesterday! We need to see how to walk this all out. The world has been so full of plastic people, hiding everything they do which they feel will cause them judgment or worst of all rejection. Stop trying to measure up to others and stop telling yourself you are too old! Whatever your excuse is, stop it right now!

God gives us some incredible commands and we can use them to prophesy over our lives, for example:

I am a conqueror and I will overcome the enemy as I cast him under my feet. I will stand on this rock (Jesus) and the gates of hell will not prevail. I will keep my eyes on Jesus and I will not look to the left or to the right and I will prosper everywhere I go. God, I thank you for empowering me with the ability to meditate on your word. Your word will not depart from out of my mouth! I will meditate on your Word day and night and as I obey your Word, you will make my way prosperous and teach me to deal wisely and to have great success. I will be strong, vigorous, and courageous. I will not be afraid nor be dismayed because you, Almighty God, are with me everywhere I go.

God commanded them to go through the camp, to prepare their provisions and to pass over the camp. What if that is to get rid of baggage we have been carrying? We keep picking up the past or stuff that is not ours to carry as a burden and I believe this is what God wants us to give to Him.

An amazing Power Evangelist, an incredible man of God, spoke to our class at GSSM while I was attending and I remember him showing us scripture that talks about our past no longer being ours. If you look at scripture, sometimes it is not what is written but what is not written.

For example, in the Scriptures below, the future and our present are mentioned ("death nor life") however, our past is not mentioned.

Romans 8:38-39 (Amp)

For I am persuaded beyond doubt (am sure) that neither death nor life, nor angels nor principalities, nor things impending and threatening nor things to come, nor powers, nor height nor depth, nor anything else in all creation will be able to separate us from the love of God which is in Christ Jesus our Lord.

1 Corinthians 3:22 (Amp)

Whether Paul or Apollos or Cephas (Peter), or the universe or life or death, or the immediate and threatening present or the [subsequent and uncertain] future—all are yours

The past is not listed in either of these two scriptures. **Romans 8:38-39** explains to us that nothing can separate us from the love of God. When we are baptized, it is our old man that is dead and the past is gone. We, as humans, sometimes have trouble letting it go. The Holy Spirit is in us to empower us to stay away from the past. The Scripture from **1 Corinthians** shows us what is ours, and again why is the past left out? Is it because the past is no longer ours (Jesus paid for it on the Cross) and when God tells Joshua not to turn to the left hand nor the right hand and that in doing so he will prosper. The key is to not look even to the side but to stay focused on what lies straight ahead.

I was in church a few years ago when an amazing farmer and grandpa in our church spoke. He shared about plowing the fields. When you plow the fields, if you take your hands off the plow to look back, you start to plow where you don't belong. If start focused on the end of your plow row you will stay the course, plowing in a straight line. We can't take our eyes off of Jesus in front of us, because if you plow in the wrong place, I believe people get hurt. If you sow seed in the wrong location or in soil that is not good, you won't be prosperous. It is vital to know the Father and what He is saying for each moment of our walk with Him. Jesus only did what the Father did and only went where the Father went; this only comes with an intimate relationship with the Father, Jesus, and the Holy Spirit.

Where is the
Body of Christ Today?

Where is the Body of Christ today? Lots of people struggle to know where we are and where we are heading. I want to unravel some things God has been showing me to give you some points to ponder and some meat to chew on.

Do you ever wonder why when we accept Jesus, we are like this live wire running around half-crazed and wanting to witness to everyone? Some of us may be the transformed person who withdraws from our old friends because we can't relate to them anymore or we sometimes even fear that we may get drawn back into behaving like or being "the old us". I came across some really interesting scripture and I would love to unfold it.

Isaiah 59:15-21

"The Lord was displeased that there was no justice. He saw there was no one, and He was appalled that there was no one to intervene. So His own arm worked salvation for Him, and His own righteousness sustained Him."

"He put on the breastplate of righteousness, the helmet of salvation, put on garments of vengeance, and wrapped himself in zeal as in a cloak."

Isaiah 40:10

"Sovereign Lord comes with power and his arm rules for him"

This makes perfect sense: when we are saved, we are wrapped in the Zeal of the Lord, we are given the helmet of salvation, and the breastplate of righteousness and God has his vengeance because He has redeemed us from the enemy. His great vengeance is to see those who come against us come to know Him also. Now that is the vengeance in my book!

We run 100 mph in the direction for God, and yes, we are new Christians with little or no wisdom! God doesn't say "stop running", He says to ask for wisdom! Whereas the Church says for us to slow down and get educated. When did the Disciples slow down? They were educated as they walked life out with Jesus. They didn't wait until they got the four-point Sermon on how and how not to minister. They also stumbled and many times Jesus just shook his head at their lack of faith. Other times He sent them back out, to go ahead of Him like "lambs among wolves". They wanted to call down fire on a town that refused to receive Jesus and for that they were corrected by Jesus. He didn't give them a time out or wait years for them to get it right. He continued to allow them to walk beside Him and even go out ahead of Him. This is completely upside down to the way we are taught. Their lack of faith and heart alignment did not cause Jesus any struggles,

He just kept walking with them and teaching them (even Judas the deceiver). Jesus still loved them even with their fighting amongst themselves as to whose miracles were better or who was going to get to sit beside Jesus in the Kingdom! They walked it out and through walking it out, they learned. Although we do not have Jesus physically walking with us, we do have the Holy Spirit to teach us as we go.

Just as in Isaiah, the Lord wants us to shine our lights brightly once we have invited Him into our hearts and surrendered our lives to Him.

Isaiah 60:1-4

Arise, shine, for your light has come, and the glory of the LORD rises upon you. See, darkness covers the earth and thick darkness is over the peoples; but the LORD rises upon you and His glory appears over you. Nations will come to your light, and kings to the brightness of your dawn. Lift up your eyes and look about you: All assemble and come to you; your sons come from afar, and your daughters are carried on the hip."

The Spirit of God went into Ezekiel and it raised him to his feet. When the Spirit of God comes into us, we should be empowered by the Love, the power, and the authority of Jesus Christ. We are okay in Church or even on the streets with people praying a prayer. I believe we are in a culture that thinks it is okay to just pray a prayer and their lives are all changed. However, we don't read that in scripture and this amazing book of Ezekiel is a guide to help us walk into the heart of the Father. The Word of God then tells Ezekiel that the people are "obstinate and stubborn and won't listen to Him when He speaks". In the Hebrew this means: hard, difficult, severe, and even fierce. The part of this scripture that caught my attention was that even though the people may not listen to Ezekiel, they would "know that a prophet had been among them."

Ezekiel 2:1-3

He said to me, "Son of man stand up on your feet and I will speak to you." As he spoke, the Spirit came into me and raised me to my feet, and I heard him speaking to me. He said: "Son of man, I am sending you to the Israelites, to a rebellious nation that has rebelled against me; they and their ancestors have been in revolt against me to this very day.

Ezekiel 2:4-7

The people to whom I am sending you are obstinate and stubborn. Say to them, 'This is what the Sovereign LORD says.' And whether they listen or fail to listen—for they are a rebellious people—they will know that a prophet has been among them. And you, son of man, do not be afraid of them or their words. Do not be afraid, though briers and thorns are all around you and you live among scorpions. Do not be afraid of what they say or be terrified by them, though they are a rebellious people. You must speak my words to them, whether they listen or fail to listen, for they are rebellious.

God took me into the heart of Ezekiel one day and in just the first few Chapters it wrecked me for more of God. The second Chapter of Ezekiel was a place God used to speak to me about how the Spirit of God moved Ezekiel.

The church needs to be empowered by the Holy Spirit to go where the Father is to do His will. God told Ezekiel to not be afraid, to listen to what He had to say, to not rebel and to open his mouth and eat what God was giving him (Ezekiel 2:8-9). We need to understand how important those words from God may be to someone else; they may break off someone's chains from the enemy. What if you chose to not speak to that person? What happens then? Ezekiel three gives an example of what can happen. When God asks us to speak to someone, we need to understand that we should walk in reverential fear of God. I know we walk under grace, but I also believe we are held accountable for every single thing which we are given. Ezekiel was told (Ezekiel 3: 18-19 and Ezekiel 3:20-21) that if he doesn't share with someone when God asks him to and that person dies, their blood is on the hands of Ezekiel! Wow, those words should put reverential fear of the Lord in us! When I first read those words in Ezekiel, they really hit me!

Ezekiel 3:18-19

When I say to a wicked person, 'You will surely die', and you do not warn them or speak out to dissuade them from their evil ways in order to save their life, that wicked person will die for their sin, and I will hold you accountable for their blood. But if you do warn the wicked person and they do not turn from their wickedness or from their evil ways, they will die for their sin; but you will have saved yourself.

Ezekiel 3:20-21

Again, when a righteous person turns from their righteousness and does evil, and I put a stumbling block before them, they will die. Since you did not warn them, they will die for their sin. The righteous things that person did will not be remembered, and I will hold you accountable for their blood. But if you do warn the righteous person not to sin and they do not sin, they will surely live because they took warning, and you will have saved yourself.

When I look at Ezekiel 2, I see that when the Spirit of the Lord came upon Ezekiel, it stood him to his feet. It gave him the ability to stand tall and took him from a seated position to a "ready to go" position. The Holy Spirit helped to change his position for the season he was about to walk into. We need the Holy Spirit to stand us up and to prepare us to be in position where we are called and to stand firm upon the words God is giving us to stand on. Throughout the Book of Acts it speaks of the importance of the Baptism of the Holy Spirit. There are many examples given in the Book of Acts about how people receive this Baptism of the Holy Spirit, making it clear that there is no set way people receive the Holy Spirit. I am not saying we don't get a measure of the Spirt when we first receive Jesus. I am talking about the actual Baptism of the Holy Spirit. I challenge you to read through the entire book of Acts and look for the different outpourings of the Baptism of the Holy Spirit to help you better understand the importance of going after this in our own lives and for other people's lives. What if the Baptism of the Holy spirit is what actually gives people the power to walk out their salvation? We wonder why people can't straighten up their lives after they say a simple prayer. We think that the "Sinner's Prayer for Salvation" is all that is needed.

Let's start with Jesus breathing on the Disciples in John 21 and saying "receive the Holy Spirit". Welcome the Comforter! In Acts 1:2, Scripture states that they received instructions through the Holy Spirit. Jesus said "receive power when the Holy Spirit comes on you and you will be my witnesses ... and to the end of the earth." In this Scripture it once again talks about a "power" that will give you the ability to proclaim the gospel. Unfortunately, we see very little power within the Body of Christ and it makes me wonder why?! Scripture also says "it is not (for us) to know the times or dates the Father has set by His own authority", so why are we so obsessed with trying to figure out when Jesus is going to return? If we would stop trying to get Jesus to come back to snatch us out of this "horrific life" and instead start to focus on the Jesus that lives inside of us and pray for the Baptism of the Holy Spirit to come upon us to give us the power to walk out our destiny, I feel we would really see the Body of Christ come into alignment with the heart of the Father and the nations would begin to see healing.

As the Disciples were praying and about the Father's business, a "suddenly" came in Acts 2 with a great outpouring of the Holy Spirit. The Spirit of God is not just for some, but for all ages and all genders and all races. Peter talks about the importance of dreams and visions and most importantly prophecy. What if we really walked so in tune with the Father and Jesus, so filled with the Spirit, that we would really start to speak life into others and see them set free, delivered, healed, and their hope would be restored and they also would be on fire for God? I think we would see what the early Church in Acts saw when they saw 3,000 people added to their numbers in just one day and they increased in size daily. What could that look like?

While on an outreach through the prophetic and through love, we saw God give Words of Knowledge about people's injuries in a really rough neighborhood where people needed to experience the tangible presence of God. Each person on the porch was healed and set free to the degree that one man had a shoulder injury which the Lord gave a Word of Knowledge about and the man kept asking "how did you know?" When I said that God showed me that he had shoulder pain, he was still in disbelief. The man was healed and set free of the effects of PTSD and anger issues. How cool was it to see the move of God touch everyone on that porch, not leaving anyone out? This move of God continued across the street onto to another porch! The most awesome thing was standing on the porch, speaking life into a man and having him say to me: "I want to know this God you know". He asked about how he could know the God I know!

I surprised myself when I said these words: "You already know Him, but the people who prayed for you didn't pray for the Baptism of Holy Spirit so you could receive the power to walk out your salvation". Wow! he asked me to pray for him. As we were ministering, another man stepped up onto the porch. This man had the lingo and verbiage to put the best of the best revival tent Pastors to shame; I believe this young man and the words he spoke could have an entire tent of people on their faces at a Revival Tent Meeting. There was only one small problem: he was strung out on drugs! I asked him if he had a lower back problem and he replied "yes!" God touched lives on both sides of the street that day.

Just as the Rulers of the Law in Acts 4:13 were astonished by the boldness and confidence they saw demonstrated by uneducated, ordinary men. These men could see that they had been with Jesus! I am excited for the Body of Christ to walk in such a way that we really do emulate Jesus because we Are His reflection in the world today. When will we walk with Jesus in the full measure of His joy? What seems to be missing in the Body of Christ that God is putting on your heart to do differently [What are the Shepherds doing? Are they doing the will of their Father?]

God says we can judge the fruit of others and when I hear others say they equip people, but still see the same old thing as yesterday, I shake my head. God keeps taking me back to the Scriptures and showing me areas like in Nehemiah where the ministering priests, worshipers and the gatekeepers were provided a place to stay. Nehemiah said "We will not neglect the house of our God" (Nehemiah 10:39). Later within the Book of Nehemiah this all gets changed when Nehemiah leaves for a season and things were under another person's responsibility. Everything changed and the the worshipers and Levites who where responsible for the services had actually gone back to working their own fields because the portion assigned to them previously was no longer being given to them. I understand that as ministries are created and just becoming established, this is really hard to do because of the lack of finances and the lack of room to house people - that is not what I am talking about. I struggle with understanding God's balance because I saw within the Scriptures the importance of worshipers and I feel that the "gatekeepers" could represent some of our important intercessors. I do not know how to walk this all out, but I felt God is highlighting this area within the Body of Christ. In Nehemiah 13:11, Nehemiah rebuked the officials and asked them this important question: "Why is the house of God neglected?" I feel God is saying something deeper in these Scriptures and it goes along with the following Scripture in Ezekiel.

Ezekiel 34:1-6

The word of the LORD came to me: "Son of man, prophesy against the shepherds of Israel; prophesy and say to them: 'This is what the Sovereign LORD says: Woe to you shepherds of Israel who only take care of yourselves! Should not shepherds take care of the flock? You eat the curds, clothe yourselves with the wool and slaughter the choice animals, but you do not take care of the flock. You have not strengthened the weak or healed the sick or bound up the injured. You have not brought back the strays or searched for the lost. You have ruled them harshly and brutally. So they were scattered because there was no shepherd, and when they were scattered they became food for all the wild animals. My sheep wandered over all the mountains and on every high hill. They were scattered over the whole earth, and no one searched or looked for them.

These Scriptures point out where the church has been. I feel God is saying we are slowly coming out of this dark age and into the understanding of Sonship. I struggled for years after God showed me these Scriptures and I have been holding on to this revelation for quite a few years. I couldn't understand why the pastors and leaders of large ministries would say one things like: "we are an equipping center", but I really only saw a few people being launched out on their own into ministry. I am starting to see that we only teach what we have been taught. When I see something differently, I am responsible for what I am given and not what someone else is doing.

I have an amazing friend whom God used to help open my eyes. I would experience anger and frustration running me around a flag pole when I would see these things, and she helped me to see that "they are only doing what they know". I saw that a Pastor who had been in ministry for about 30 years is only just now walking out some things in his life that I started to walk out a few years ago. I shook my head in disbelief, but God showed me that He is only just bringing His leaders out into a new season where they will be ready to be diligent with the beginning stages of what everyone calls the "Billion Soul Harvest". Bob Jones who was an incredible

Prophet spoke of the Billion Soul Harvest and shared that God sent him back from death to touch a few of the leaders that God will use during that Harvest. I believe that millions of leaders are needed to be raised up that look at ministry differently; they will need to be "Upside Down Kingdom" men and women. I now see the beginnings of that happening across the world, where you see people actually empowering others and launching them in to their destinies. If you, as a leader, have not helped to open doors for others, I question whether you really have empowered the Body of Christ. I was not a mother in the natural, but sometimes when we don't have something, the longing in our spirit is greater. Sometimes when we didn't see something happen in our own lives, God will use that to catapult us into position to be used in ways we have not been taught by man. Such as the way God is opening doors for me in ministry where man never opened doors for me, and I am now in a position to help to launch others through those same doors.

Even if I am unable to walk through a door myself, will I open it for someone else I believe God is using? Will I help empower someone who has struggled in life and call out their greatness? Will I give grace where I never saw grace when God prompts me to be more gracious? Do I really trust God more than I trust myself, is that really what it all comes down to? Will I be the quarter in God's pocket to be spent any way He chooses?

I pray this stirs your heart to go after answers in your own life. I am not here to point fingers, nor am I hear to tell you how it is all done. I believe that if we would all listen to God, it would look different for each of us. God can use an ex-drug dealer to reach a really rough area but he could also choose to use a person like Heidi Baker to reach out to a rough area and both of these people could be used by Him. Looking at life without allowing our experiences to hinder the way we walk forward is a huge key. Allowing what people say to take you deeper into the heart of the Father for confirmation is also a key factor. We need others in our lives, but they do not have the final say on how we walk out our life. When you stand before God, those people who are around you now will not be standing beside you. You will not be able to say, "they told me to do this or that". You will be responsible for yourself and no one else but yourself. We need to live our lives by looking at life in this way: If Jesus was standing before you in this moment, what would you be saying or doing? An incredible ministry partner says that all the time and I love it and have started to use that in my daily walk with Jesus. Would I say some of the things I say while standing before God or would I do some of the things I do if I was actually physically standing before Jesus?

If Scripture is correct and John 17 is truth, Jesus and God live inside of us and we might want to start caring more about how we walk out our lives. I am also a work in progress, and my measuring stick is that I want to be in a better place tomorrow than I am standing in today!

Song of Solomon 5 Revelation

As God took me on this journey of unveiling more of what He was showing me about the Body of Christ and where the Western Church is and isn't, I continued to ask questions because it was hitting my heart severely. I felt called by God to go to a Church on the evening before the Day of Atonement to spend the night in that Church, praying. During this time, God had me read the entire Book of the Song of Solomon. God got my attention in a major way through Chapter 5 and has taken me back to that Scripture many times since.

The Scripture in Song of Solomon 5:3-6 really concerns me for the Body of Christ. What if this is where the Church Body is at this moment in time? What if we are too busy to answer the door when our lover, Jesus, comes knocking? Will we answer in the same way when we just took off our robe? Will we not want to put it back on to go to the door? Will we have just washed our feet and not want to soil them again, so we won't go to the door to answer when He comes? Will His scent draw us, but will it be after He has already left? I know the ending of the story is where she is back with her lover and that is very exciting. What if we are to be an example so others can follow us?

My prayer is that each of us seek out the posture of our own heart and allow God to speak to you on the areas God is highlighting for us to address. I feel I am writing some of this to stir your heart to take it all back to God to let Him give you His revelation and heart for you!

Wedding Banquet Revelation

Another revelation God gave me happened one day while I was sitting in a United Methodist Church. The Pastor has been an amazing friend and pastor to me over the last 8 years; He has honored me as I have grown in Christ and blessed me. I was sitting in his service one Sunday and he was talking about the Wedding Banquet. This has been an area that I have been camping out in for quite a while, trying to understand who the person is that has no wedding garment on. I have had this on my heart for some time because I believe the Church is in this very place and God has been speaking to me about the shape of the Bride, His Church! As I was intently listening and enjoying what God was speaking through the Pastor, I felt the prompting of the Holy Spirit to look up the Greek word for Wedding Garment discussed in Matthew 22:1-13.

The Father wants to have a Wedding Banquet for His Son and sends out His servants to invite guests to the banquet. The people invited are not interested or have "more important" things going on in their lives and they decline, making their excuses for not attending the Wedding Banquet. Their excuses are: one tending to his field, another to his business, and the rest of the people invited seize His servants, mistreating and even killing them. While the Banquet is being prepared, the King sends out more servants to gather all the people they can find on the Highways and the Byways. They are instructed to get the good and the bad. They are to fill the Wedding Hall with guests. When the King comes in to see the guests, He notices one man not wearing a Wedding Garment! The King has this man bound hand and foot and taken away and casts him into the "darkness where there shall be weeping and gnashing of teeth."

When I looked it up in the concordance, the Wedding Garment in the Greek is the same word for Outer Garment! It is the same word used for the Outer Garment that Peter puts on to dive into the water as he returns to Jesus who is waiting to feed him breakfast on the shore after Peter had denied Jesus three times. It is the same word, so it has to have the same meaning! What if this person who I have been trying to figure out whether is good and bad, is a person who says they are a Christian, but there is not any fruit in their life?

What if this person thinks they can slide through, unnoticed in life, as a Christian in name only? This grips my heart in a way that scares me! That is who I was before God pulled my car off the embankment so many years ago; I was a Christian in name only. That could also be many people I know today. I am not judging. I am just really concerned because of what I feel God is revealing to me; the more I come into agreement with the Heart of the Father, the more my heart breaks for the Body of Christ where many still do not have an active relationship with all three members of the Trinity.

What does Reformation look like today?

God has been creating a burning in my heart to see where His heart is for the Body of Christ. He has taken me on a journey over the past few years. Each time God shows me something, it breaks my heart more and more which in turn causes me to seek out His heart even more.

God has shown me Scriptures that grip my heart with brokenness because I know where I was for 18 years as a "so-called" Christian. I wonder now, would I have gone to heaven on the day I tried to commit suicide? How much of my life would I have missed out on? Then I thought of my destiny in the Lord! Was I even walking in my destiny? Would I have left a legacy that would help others walk into their destiny? Probably not!

I had always believed the concept of "Once Saved Always Saved!" I am not 100% convinced of that today. God says that no one will snatch you out of His hand, but what about you yourself walking out of His hand? I did have incredible faith that if I died I would go to heaven! I do know that I was deeply moved emotionally on the day I received Jesus as my Lord and Savior as a 20-year-old. During those 18 years of that Christian walk, did I somehow unknowingly walk out of His will? That is what I would like to ask you to seek out within your life- are you walking within the center of the destiny that the Lord has for you?

I have started asking God questions all the time. Questions like: How do I finish this race well? What is the race I am running? Who am I? What is my purpose in life? How do I walk in the fullness of what You have for me in my life? How can I leave a legacy for others to see how to walk out their own destinies?

I had many questions and for quite a while, very few answers. God showed me that my identity is not found in man or other things (like my job). My identity can't be created by what I do or where I go. The key to understand my identity was to know and understand Who lives inside of me and Whose I am. Learning more about God, Jesus, and the Holy Spirit that abide in me was the beginning of me understanding my true identity. I saw the lack of this training in the Church firsthand. How can I learn was my question? God took me through a series of steps in my learning process. He would show me Scriptures that would rend my heart and then I would hear speakers that would give me pieces of golden nuggets that fit together like a puzzle. The greatest part of this journey in seeking understanding of my true identity has been the journey with Him.

Before He "died", Jesus said that we will do the things He did and even greater things. Everything started with fire and excitement as His Church began in Acts 2. Now when you look out across the Body of Christ (Church), you don't really see the Power and Authority of God moving in the Church Body for the most part.

Jesus is the key to our walk in life and ministry and He has given us so much to unpack. What if what the world says is Peter being reinstated and forgiven is really Jesus actually showing Peter how to Shepard those he will lead?

What if through John 21, Jesus is helping us to understand leadership in ministry and we can even use it in our own lives.

John 21:5-19

⁵ When they had finished eating, Jesus said to Simon Peter, "Simon son of John, do you love me more than these?" "Yes, Lord," he said, "you know that I love you." Jesus said, "Feed my lambs."

¹⁶ Again Jesus said, "Simon son of John, do you love me?" He answered, "Yes, Lord, you know that I love you." Jesus said, "Take care of my sheep."

¹⁷ The third time he said to him, "Simon son of John, do you love me?" Peter was hurt because Jesus asked him the third time, "Do you love me? "He said, "Lord, you know all things; you know that I love you." Jesus said, "Feed my sheep.

¹⁸ Very truly I tell you, when you were younger you dressed yourself and went where you wanted; but when you are old you will stretch out your hands, and someone else will dress you and lead you where you do not want to go."¹⁹ Jesus said this to indicate the kind of death

by which Peter would glorify God. Then he said to him, "Follow me!"

Jesus asks Peter does he love him and Peter responds with a "yes" each time. Each time Jesus asks, the word Love he used represented a different type of Love within the translation of the words He used for love. Jesus says in the first Scriptures for Peter to "feed my lambs". Feeding a lamb is unique and what I have read shows they have different sets of teeth as they grow. Could it be possible that new Christians need to be fed so they are able to chew the "meat" after they are weaned from the milk which they need as brand new lambs. There seem to be five different stages in the learning process for Christians. As a leader or Shepherd, I would need to know each member of my flock specifically and to really know them and the level where they are in their spiritual walk in order to be certain they are fed the right food.

When you move into the next group of Scriptures, Jesus says, "Take care of my Sheep". What if we actually need to spend time with people to get to know them and then we can know where they are having breakthrough and where they are struggling. God is all about relationship and His heart is being in our lives fully and constantly. He gives us what we need to make our own choices in life without going against our will. How can we do this in our lives and know the people around us without being discouraged with their walk of life? How can we grow in grace and freely give it to others when needed while also giving correction and exhortation to help set them on the correct course of life as Christians when needed?

Within the last section of Scripture, Jesus says "Feed my Sheep". We can't feed something or someone without knowing what their need is or how to reach them. It all goes back to understanding who we are responsible for in our walk of life, as well as how do we help them get to the next season of their life without cutting out the stoney path for them. We can be used by God to help them, but ultimately they need to do the work for their own lives. The work they need is to find the heart of the Father in their life and to understand that their life is so precious and so valued that Jesus came just for them and them alone. We spread ourselves so far and wide sometimes that too many people get lost in the cracks of life. How can we help raise up the leader in others to become the true Body of Christ? What is your role in this part of life and who are you empowering? Don't say that is not your call. I think it is for all of us; Jesus commissioned us all and if Jesus lives inside of you there is nothing holding you back and there is nothing impossible for you in the task set before you. After Jesus says all that, He has one more command for Peter. Jesus says: "Follow me!" Peter followed unto death, upside down upon a Cross. I would like to propose that in that moment, Peter was transformed into the Rock and against this Rock the gates of hell did not prevail.

The Difference Between Moses and Pharaoh

Have you ever thought about how two people raised in the same family and raised as brothers could be so different? There are two characters in the Bible I would like to talk about: Moses and Pharaoh. They were both raised in the same house. Two people raised in the same house, but their hearts were in two totally different places. I would like to take you on a journey to show you some revelations God showed me about these two men.

Exodus 4:21

"And the Lord said to Moses, when you return into Egypt, see that you do before Pharaoh all those miracles and wonders which I have put in our hand; but I will make him stubborn and harden his heart, so that he will not let the people go."

Exodus 10:27

"But Jehovah hardened Pharaoh's heart, and he would not let them go."

What was in Pharaoh's heart? When God hardened his heart, what was in Pharaoh's heart? The Hebrew word for hardened is ***chazaq***, meaning to strengthen, to press. I would like to propose that when the glory of God falls on us, whatever is within us is strengthened. This can be a serious problem when we refuse to let God have our heart 100%.

God says He has given us free will and He will not force His will on us. We are free to choose to follow Him. We have to choose to be obedient to Him. We also choose whether to allow Him into our hearts fully, half-heartedly, or not at all. All of this is our own choice due to free will.

My heart is that I want to continue to run the race God has for me. That means laying down anything and everything that He shows me that will hinder my walk, especially what is not of Him. We need to routinely ask God to search our hearts to reveal anything and everything not of Him so we can allow His fullness to abide in us. He can only abide in the areas we give up! I know for me it has been a process and I am still being processed every day.

James 1:13 tells us:

"When tempted, no one should say, "God is tempting me." For God cannot be tempted by evil, nor does He tempt anyone;"

If that is the case, God may use what is inside of us to work it out of us as we go through trials, but God Himself is not tempting you. What if God already knew the heart of Pharaoh and had already tried to pour out over him? We don't know! What if God decided to pour out one more time and He knew the outcome and would use that outcome to set the stage to free the captives. Pharaoh wasn't willing to lose all the Israelites. They were his workers who got the job done because he had control over them! Who would do the work if they lost their slaves?

Let's take these scriptures into our culture today and see what that might look like in our lives. We can see many businesses in the world where people control their workforce through fear and use their power and authority to force their employees into working harder and harder, being a slave (in a sense) to their every command. These people really have no say and the harder they work, the more work is required of them. It is a never ending battle where they find themselves at the bottom of the pile of work that is placed on top of them. You fear speaking out because you need the income! You fear taking a stand, because you could lose your job! You fret and worry, striving to get more work done even start to take it home with you! It starts to consume your every thought and if you don't bring it home physically, you do emotionally. You are bound by your work, by your employer, and it spiritually starts to kill you. We become slaves in our own lives!

I was there once and it actually drove me to suicide. I was so riddled with pain, especially in the years immediately prior to my suicide attempt. I wanted to be loved and accepted and I set out to succeed at my career. I soon found I couldn't please my boss or the company because I was in a field that involved computers and part of my job was removing viruses from the computers. It was a time when you would fix them one day and the same virus would show up the next day and it seemed were chasing your own tail. No solution to the viruses worked long term! No happy co-workers; no happy Boss; no happy company. It was especially tough when you worked in several different offices and you were a person who needed approval from others to feel good about yourself.

In looking at Pharaoh's life, was he mean and controlling and used to using force to get his kingdom running his way? What kind of person would hold people against their will by being beaten down and belittled? Slavery is holding and forcing people against their will by force. Was it done through love, honor, or respect? Not likely. Look at the man who Moses killed because of the way the Israelite was being beaten by him. Seeing this mistreatment of a slave angered Moses to the point where he killed the man and then had to flee.

God says we are responsible for what we are given! Do different ingredients create different products when going through the fire? What about Clay and Concrete? Clay would melt yet concrete would harden!

The Israelites finally started to cry out to God because they finally got tired of the place where the enemy had them, and they started to pray! They cried out to God and He knew that Pharaoh's heart would not free them and so His mighty hand was needed to remove their bondage, setting the captives free.

Are there parts of your heart that you haven't given up to God yet? Ask God to search it every day and to show you the areas you have not yet surrendered to him and where the strongholds are that hinder your freedom. God will show you and guide you as you ask Him. My heart is not to be the person who is sitting on the couch someday wondering "what if" questions about my life, never having moved anywhere and never having stepped into my destiny.

God spoke to me about a few years ago as I was traveling across the country to attend a leadership school. I was already in ministry full time for several years at this point and couldn't understand what God was doing, sending me to another leadership school. Sometimes we feel we know better than God does for our own lives (NOT)! As I was talking with God on my long journey, I heard God clearly say these words to me: "I am building character in you to sustain the dream so the dream doesn't crush you". That will get you to thinking!

I want to end this book on this note. We think we know because we see something or dream about it. Really! God shows us stuff and it usually is only the tip of the iceberg to what He has for our lives because we would really screw it up or run like a little school girl scared to death. Either way, we probably would not fulfill our destiny if it was only in our hands. God knows there are areas of my life I need to give Him fully before He can give me the open doors for the dreams for my life to fully manifest.

One key component for my character development was a meeting with an overseer of the school. He was helping me to walk through some stuff I was dealing with and took me back to the deliverance I had in 2015 and my wholeness process where God gave me a dream. In the dream God gave me, He showed me my Dad yelling at my Mom when I was the little tiny baby in the crib off to my right. I remember the room all too well: it was my parents' bedroom in the house I grew up in. My Dad was yelling to my Mom to please shut me up. I remember my Mom telling me that I came home from the hospital sick for the first three months of my life with a staph ear infection that the doctors could not find. I was really sick with high fevers and they would rub me down with alcohol to try to bring the fevers down. The fevers even affected the enamel on my secondary teeth. I didn't see what my Mom did when my Dad yelled at her to please shut me up, but I remembered that scene all too well. I know that in that moment, the enemy (not my parents) attacked a little defenseless baby girl who just needed to be loved and for the pain to go away. Nothing more and nothing less. But my parents were unable to help because they too had no answers in the heat of the summer with no help from the doctors and a father who worked hard outside to put food on the table for his family of seven. Any father would have a breaking point. Any father would be at a loss for lack of sleep and rest. In those moments, the enemy, not my parents attacked a little defenseless baby girl and created yet another wound that this time medicine would not be able to fix. This time the wound would go deep into her spirit and cause her to believe she was unloved. The term "unloved" means that you once felt loved and I came from an amazing loving family. They may or may not have dealt with life always in love, but did everything because of love. In those moments, a little baby started to recieve the lie of being unloved. During my inner healing meeting while at the leadership school, I gained a greater understanding that in that moment, I also learned that I could not trust my Mom to protect me and ultimately learned that I couldn't trust my Dad and because of that I was unable to fully trust God. Trust issues surfaced and slapped me in the face when I was asked "what was my relationship with my Mom?" I had an awesome friendship with my Mom and we had been best friends since my Dad had died when I was 15. When I heard the words "you could be best friends with your mom, but I bet you were unable to receive from her" touch my ears, I was undone by uncontrollable tears. I loved my Mom the best way I knew how, but there really was always a wall between us and at times it was a love/hate relationship. Through the process, I learned I didn't trust very well and I have been on a journey ever since, learning how to trust God with every aspect of my life. That little girl grew up to be a very independent woman and the enemy used leader after leader to hold me back or destroy me in different ways, reinforcing my lack of trust. Most times they didn't do anything directly to cause me to not trust, but the enemy always directed my eyes to see where they had failed. I learned through the lies that I could not trust leaders to protect me or even the people close to me. That is not a good place to walk; It can get very lonely walking that place out, because you ultimately don't even trust the one you think you trust, and that is God. I have had incredible healing since that meeting and still to this day am learning how to walk out trust when I don't feel trusting. Ultimately, do we trust God, even if we don't trust the people around us? That is the actual issue! If we trust God, we will not care if others protect us or have our best interest at heart. If we fully trust God, we will know He has our best interests at heart and He is our protector. That year was an incredible year of learning to trust and it happened quickly.

The school was a 9-month school and it was with a well known ministry. Of course you want to finish it, especially when you have incredible friends and family members sowing into your education. My next challenge was about to unfold. If God says leave school early and leave unoffendable, will you walk out obedience? I was tested to my very core. I learned early on that God sees things differently than we do and that what God does is not always seen as wisdom by the world. Look at Moses and how he had to walk out his test of faith. In the obedience of my faith, I walked out leaving school seven weeks early without graduating, however, it actually set me up to be used in an incredible way. I had the opportunity to join up with another friend to pour into an amazing Brazilian friend and where three friends ventured all across the USA on a seven-week journey. The journey was not always easy and we didn't always know what it looked like financially.

However, the end result was us raising the money for our Brazilian friend to attend another amazing ministry school for three weeks where she actually met her husband and was married a short period of time later. My graduation day from the leadership school I left early was the first day of my Brazilian friend's school registration over 3,000 miles away. Would you have left a well known ministry leadership school out of obedience to God not knowing why? I am so glad I left when I did and was available to help my friend when she was actually in desperate need of help. When you walk out obedience, it may or may not look like God. You need to have a relationship with God the Father, Jesus the Son, and the Holy Spirit the Comforter in order to know when it is God and when it isn't God. Yes, they are all the same God, but they all operate differently in and through our lives.

As you walk out your destiny there are several things to make note of in your life:

- Am I open to being taught by God and others?
- Will I allow God to open up my heart and "fillet" it so He can remove the roots of the lies I have been believing all my life, even from the womb?
- Will you lay down your life as Jesus gave His life to be fully possessed by God to see the full manifestation of Jesus in your life where you will see the Father and you will know where the Father is at all times because He becomes one inside of you as Jesus is one with the Father (John 17)?

And my last question: will you let God take you places you never dreamed of or do things in and through your life you never thought of to reach just one person? Your life could be to just reach one person! Are you ok to be used to reach just one person, because if you are in that place to be used by God as that quarter in His pocket to spend you any way He wants, you will be undone by the relationship you will have with God more than anything else in your life. Really, nothing else matters but to love God and be loved by God and out of that love you will be able to "love the hell" out of others and stomp Hell!

Will you be a deliverer as Moses was or will you be delivered into the waves of the enemy like Pharoah? Your choice!

Are you ready to be "unleashed and ready to empower" with Jesus? Will you allow yourself to be Unleashed to Empower others?

References

References are taken from the Bible (NIV, KJV, Amplified, and Passion Translations)

Difference sheep and lamb
http://www.differencebetween.net/science/nature/difference-between-lambs-and-sheep/

Photo credit to Trina Olson – painting called Unleashed and Ready to Reign

Editing Credits:
Donna Emidy for the first round of Editing

Edith Houghton Chapman follow on Editing

Thank you both, I couldn't have finished it without your help!

About the Author

Trina Olson is an Itinerant Minister and founder of Radical Launch International Ministries, Inc. and Co-founder of Unleashed Publishing, Inc. She received her ordination through Randy Clark's Global School of Supernatural Ministries and The Apostolic Network of Global Awakening. She has also studied under Lou Engle at Ekballo School. She attended Iris Leadership School in 2016-2017 school year. She has traveled the majority of the states in the US and been on extended trips to Brazil, Costa Rica, Nicaragua, Mexico, Dominican Republic, Guatemala, Belize, Kenya, Uganda and Malawi in just the last few years! Her Baby Blue (car) has over 400,000 miles traveling with God. Baby Blue has been donated to an incredible intercessor and friend to watch God continue to use for the Kingdom of God.

Trina's ministry, Radical Launch, reflects her heart to see others catapulted into their identity in Jesus Christ, Who will launch them into their destiny! She desires to see people encounter the one true living God through Jesus Christ, to be filled with the Holy Spirit and walk out Isaiah 61 as Jesus calls us to heal the sick, cast out demons, bind up the broken hearted, and raise the dead! She believes this is not just for a select few people, but for all! Her vision is to empower people to 'be in the game' as an important player, making a difference in the lives of everyone they encounter!

God radically transformed Trina's life in 2007 through a miraculous encounter with Himself! Her testimony is one of Divine intervention, both inner and physical healing, and victory over spirits of depression and suicide that tried to take her life. God has given her a voice and a mandate to reach the youth of America with the message of the importance and power of a personal relationship with Jesus as she shares her testimony! He literally turned her life around that day when she was committing suicide and has set a fire inside of her that has taken her on an incredible journey with Him! She believes hearing someone else's testimony sets people free from their own bondage!

Trina has a dream from God and is walking out that dream to launch others into their destiny. God is building a ministry out of relationship.

A bit of Revelation from Trina: You have a gold nugget inside of you to give to each person God puts in front of you. What you choose to do with that gold nugget is up to you. Trina learned that those gold nuggets are relationships. What if we have a part on earth in building the gold pavements of Heaven? We co-heir with Christ and if as we co-heir with Christ we love our God with all our heart, mind, spirit, and soul, and we love our neighbor as we love ourselves, the world will truly know we are Christians and hope will be restored.

Unleashed Publishing, Inc.
975 Wayne Avenue #351
Chambersburg, Pa 17201

(717) 860-1841

Unleashed Publishing, Inc. is a new publishing Company which is operating as an upside down Kingdom Business. We are about empowering a generation through launching Authors, Editors, and Illustrators into a greater freedom of expression.

Unleashed Publishing, Inc.

Unleashing the potential authors, editors, and illustrators of a generation.

Transformed
in a Moment!

Trina was transformed in a moment when God pulled her car off an embankment while committing suicide. Since that time God has led Trina on an incredible journey to reveal her true identity in Him.

Unleashed and Ready to Empower was birthed out of a vision God revealed to Trina as she was on a mission trip to Brazil in 2012. That moment led her on a journey to see herself and many others being unleashed from the limitations of the glass ceilings of life. Empowering others is a passion God has impressed upon her heart. She feels her call in life is to see a generation encounter Jesus.

Unleashed Publishing, Inc
Unleashing the potential authors, editors, and illustrators of a generation.

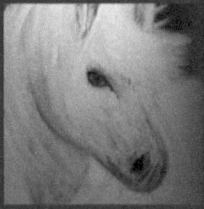

ISBN 978-1-7333090-1-1

www.ingramcontent.com/pod-product-compliance
Lightning Source LLC
Chambersburg PA
CBHW020410080526
44584CB00014B/1255